ASPATORE
Executive Business Intelligence

ASPATORE
Executive Business Intelligence

www.Aspatore.com

Aspatore is the most exclusive business book/brief/journal publisher in the world, publishing only the biggest names in the business world, including C-level leaders (CEO, CTO, CFO, COO, CMO, Partner) from over half the world's 500 largest companies and other leading executives. Aspatore publishes the Inside the Minds, Bigwig Briefs, Focusbook and Aspatore Business Review imprints in addition to other best selling business books, journals and briefs. By focusing on publishing only the biggest name executives, Aspatore provides readers with proven business intelligence from industry insiders, rather than relying on the knowledge of unknown authors and analysts. Aspatore focuses on publishing traditional print books and journals, while our portfolio company, Corporate Book Agents, focuses on developing areas within the book-publishing world. Aspatore is committed to providing our readers, authors, bookstores, distributors and customers with the highest quality books, book related services, and publishing execution available anywhere in the world.

The *Inside the Minds* Series
Real World Intelligence From Industry Insiders
www.InsideTheMinds.com

The critically acclaimed *Inside the Minds* series provides readers with proven business intelligence from C-Level executives (CEO, CFO, CTO, CMO, Partner) from the world's most respected companies. Each chapter is comparable to a white paper or essay and is a future-oriented look at where an industry/profession/topic is heading and the most important issues for future success. Each author has been carefully chosen through an exhaustive selection process by the Inside the Minds editorial board to write a chapter for this book. *Inside the Minds* was conceived in order to give readers actual insights into the leading minds of business executives worldwide. Because so few books or other publications are actually written by executives in industry, *Inside the Minds* presents an unprecedented look at various industries and professions never before available. The *Inside the Minds* series is revolutionizing the business book market by publishing an unparalleled group of executives and providing an unprecedented introspective look into the leading minds of the business world.

About Corporate Book Agents

Corporate Book Agents assists leading companies and select individuals with book writing, publisher negotiations, book publishing, book sponsorship, worldwide book promotion and generating a new revenue stream from publishing. Services also include white paper, briefing, research report, bulletin, newsletter and article writing, editing, marketing and distribution. The goal of Corporate Book Agents is to help our clients capture the attention of prospective customers, retain loyal clients and penetrate new target markets by sharing valuable information in publications and providing the highest quality content for readers worldwide. For more information please visit www.CorporateBookAgents.com or e-mail jonp@corporatebookagents.com.

INSIDE THE MINDS:
Entrepreneurial Momentum

Jump Starting a New Business Venture and Gaining Traction for Businesses of All Sizes to Take the Step to the Next Level

ASPATORE
Executive Business Intelligence

Published by Aspatore Books, Inc.
For information on bulk orders, sponsorship opportunities or any other questions please e-mail store@aspatore.com. For corrections, company/title updates, comments or any other inquiries please e-mail info@aspatore.com.

First Printing, 2002
10 9 8 7 6 5 4 3 2 1

ISBN 1-58762-214-9

Library of Congress Card Number: 2002090814

Cover design by Ian Mazie & Kara Yates

Material in this book is for educational purposes only. This book is sold with the understanding that neither any of the authors or the publisher is engaged in rendering legal, accounting, investment, or any other professional service.

This book is printed on acid free paper.

A special thanks to all the individuals that made this book possible.

Special thanks to: Jo Alice Hughes, Rinad Beidas, Kirsten Catanzano, Melissa Conradi, Molly Logan, Justin Hallberg

Acknowledgements and Dedications

From Todd Parent: To the entire Extreme Team, for your continuous hard work, dedication, and commitment to staying Extreme!
From Jack Lavin: To the founder who made this all possible: Chairman Robert L. Lavin.
From Lucinda Duncalfe Holt: For my husband, Russell, who makes my work possible, and for Frank Wilkinson, who deserves all of the credit for anything I say that sounds smart, but none of the blame for my normal blather.
From Art Feierman: To my incredible daughter Lisa, who always amazes me. To Lori, my wife and friend, and to my Mom, who still has more business sense than I do. Thanks to Vance Caesar, "the coach," and Michael Minailo, "the fundable executive."

The views expressed by the individuals in this book do not necessarily reflect the views shared by the companies they are employed by (or the companies mentioned in this book). The companies referenced may not be the same company that the individual works for since the publishing of this book.

The views expressed by the endorsements on the cover of this book for the *Inside the Minds* series do not necessarily reflect the views shared by the companies they are employed by. The companies referenced may not be the same company that the individual works for since the publishing of this book.

Inside the Minds:
Entrepreneurial Momentum

Contents

THE JOURNEY TO ENTREPRENEURSHIP: A ROADMAP FOR LANDMARK ACHIEVEMENT

DAVE CONE
Camstar
Chief Executive Officer

An Offer of Insight

The rapid ascent of today's high-tech leaders has contributed to a misconception of true entrepreneurship. While overnight successes are captivating stories, many of these rags-to-riches tales distort the important role entrepreneurs have always played in American business. So much focus is placed on those few men and women who have created empires that many people overlook entrepreneurs who are around them every day – local software programmers and developers, dentists, custom machine shops, bakeries, and other small businesses. Businesses like these are being run by people who provide valuable products and services to the community. While the entrepreneurial spirit today has become associated with technology and venture capital, we must always remember a new business can emerge from anywhere.

My background is in computers and software, so I am not turning my back on the things that have allowed me to experience a tremendous amount of personal growth and satisfaction. The exact opposite is true. Creating my own business in these challenging and complex arenas has provided me with a greater appreciation for what every businessperson goes through in their quest to achieve success and build something of value. My goal is to offer some insights from my personal experiences to those who are thinking about striking out on their own. Entrepreneurs face far too many unexpected challenges and blind curves on their journeys. I hope my experiences can help travelers create recognizable landmarks for their own business roadmaps.

Entrepreneurial Self-Assessment

There are three simple but extremely important considerations the aspiring entrepreneur should consider before jumping into a new endeavor:

1. Do you like to do what you'll be doing?
2. Are you good at it?
3. Will people pay you to do it?

When starting a new venture, many people are unprepared for how all-encompassing the business becomes. You alone are now responsible for making decisions, growing the business, attracting customers, planning, and execution. You spend almost every hour of the day considering what happens next to make the business grow. You should consider putting this kind of pressure on yourself only if you are confident you will enjoy the challenges that will undoubtedly appear. Achievement will come only with the ultimate level of engagement and commitment. Merely saying a potential business is "okay" will not be enough. Whatever avenue you're considering must stimulate you while simultaneously allowing some measure of satisfaction.

Having a particular skill or talent is important, for these skills and talents ultimately become your company's product. One of the most critical things at the formation stage of the business is accurately gauging how many potential customers will want to use your product. Having demonstrable expertise and the ability to do something or make something better than others is the best method for ensuring that customers will come and the business will generate revenue. While the customers may not come as quickly as you would like them to at first, consistently delivering the highest-quality products and services provides the greatest chance for long-term success. The success of your business in the long run depends on creating a consistent chain of customers, most of whom will find you through referrals and references.

Seizing Opportunities and Gaining Traction

Opportunity comes in different sizes and shapes. Being able to recognize an opportunity and capitalize on it is a crucial aspect of building a business. My company evolved from working with a single client who asked for help in getting its internal manufacturing and business systems installed and functioning. This single client started me in the consulting business, and from this opportunity I was able to start branching out and developing a reputation as someone who could rapidly solve complex manufacturing problems using emerging technology.

One of the keys to gaining early traction for my business was working with a large partner. As an early-stage entrepreneur, you should not be afraid of partnering with the bigger fish in your industry, particularly if you can take on small parts of jobs they don't want to do. I worked with IBM's Business Partner program and got involved with IBM salespeople who were starting to do more work with outside software vendors and implementation consultants. When they had a local customer who needed implementation assistance, IBM salespeople came to me because I understood how these new high-technology manufacturers worked. My consulting engagements had exposed me to the emerging technologies of that time, and I had extensive experience working with companies on solving the problems they encountered in the tracking and management of their manufacturing processes.

At this stage, introductions to prospective customers were incredibly important. Not only did I build professional contacts for down the road, but I was also able to work with them and get their insights on the types of solutions they needed for solving their business problems. For the early-stage entrepreneur, having this access to real customers is critical, for it allows you to design services and create solutions for real problems, increasing your odds of success dramatically. Rather than finding a theoretical solution for a possible problem, you create a solution that people already need.

First Customers and Building Your Business

While every stage of developing a business presents new obstacles, I maintain that persuading those first few customers to believe in your business will be one of the most difficult challenges an entrepreneur will face. When you are just starting out, you are not selling a company so much as you are selling yourself and trying to convince customers you have the ability to solve their problems. You need to have a compelling vision to share with them, and you need to listen. You do not need to have all of the answers for every potential customer at this point. However, if you have the answers to the problems of the first customers, you can use the experience of working with them to develop the solutions for those problems that will come up in the future.

Your first customers are a vital resource in so many ways. My first customers helped fund the development of my first software product, much like a contemporary venture capitalist would. During my consulting engagements, I had begun to notice a set of common needs and started designing a product to solve those problems. At this stage, without the capital to design products full time, I had to find potential customers who believed I knew what I was doing and would pay me for my design efforts. I approached these customers with a proposition. They would help fund the creation of the software that would address their needs. In exchange for their trust and funds, they would get a functioning solution, their investments returned, and, in some cases, the potential for royalties from future software deployments.

Fortunately, these early clients saw that our solutions could quickly and cost-effectively solve their problems. Their capital allowed me to hire programmers and construct that initial system. (Our company's current chief technical officer was one of those early programmers.) We created prototypes and rolled them out to our new and existing customers. With each successful deployment, we found another customer who would allow us to develop the product further and improve on what we had already done. While this strategy may be more difficult to execute in today's economy, entrepreneurs should still consider how they can make those first customers feel like a part of the business. Building relationships and trust with customers is particularly critical at these early stages of your business and should also be the foundation of your long-term business plans.

Attracting and Keeping Long-term Customers

Your goal in attracting and keeping customers is to solve existing, real-world problems and repeatedly execute those solutions in varying circumstances. Too many companies try to create a theoretical answer to a theoretical problem and then end up trying to convince people that they might have this problem. In my experience, this approach rarely works. Today's customers have immediate needs. To be successful, you need the ability to listen attentively to what their problems are and provide a solution.

If customers are not clear or cannot express what they need, you must ask questions and suggest solutions that help bring out that need. Frame the problem in terms and issues they can understand and problems you can solve. Assimilate what you have learned from all of your previous engagements and customers into your new products or services. Each new customer should help you evolve your business and your solution to the problem. As I mentioned, customers can also be your first seed capital, as their willingness to pay for a solution may enable you to actually build the initial prototype. Look to your customers for feedback – many times they can point out problem areas you might not have foreseen and save you valuable time and energy. They are your business's lifeblood and should be treated as allies. Every action you contemplate should be based on how you can best meet their needs.

Successful Management Techniques

Delegate

One of the hardest things for an entrepreneur is to delegate authority, but it is absolutely necessary as your business grows. Don't try to do everything yourself, for you won't have the time, the knowledge, or the expertise to handle all of the issues thrown at you. Only you know your skills and limitations and when you need help. But you still have to let others provide that help. For example, although I had the idea for the software, it was time-consuming and cost-prohibitive to code and program it myself. I hired contract programmers and mapped out what I wanted, and they did the rest. I was able to maintain the company's early cash flow through sales and consulting efforts while getting the product developed much more rapidly.

Remain in the Real World

I already mentioned one technique you should avoid, but it bears repeating. Develop your product, service, or solution around real-world problems and real-world customers. As we have seen over the past several years, too many people tried to solve theoretical problems by putting people in a room, creating a project, and then trying to apply that to customers. I call this phenomenon "blue sky development." Sustaining a successful business cannot be predicated upon convincing people they may have a particular problem, and you may have a solution. Customers quickly see when they have been sold something useless, and the word quickly gets out. Take the time to research and listen to potential customers. If your product does not address their needs, take the time to go back and look for ways to respond to those needs.

Move Forward; Look Ahead

Another technique that hurts many entrepreneurs is the knee-jerk response. Too many companies end up focusing on what everyone else is doing without looking at how their own business can change. Markets are dynamic and evolving, so change will always occur. You will see new competitors emerge, new technologies develop, and new markets come into play. Keeping your business moving forward depends on having a consistent plan and sticking with it. You should focus on managing what you do and keeping that vision moving forward. I don't mean you should ignore what's going on around you. Instead, spend the time learning how your market might be changing and what is causing it to change. Rather than following every move of your competition, think about what will happen next and create a plan to move your business smoothly in a direction that can take advantage of opportunities without sacrificing the time and investments you have already made.

Build Long-Term Value

Creating a usable and repeatable architecture is crucial in the software industry, but the same logic applies to any business. The common denominator is finding and solving the problems your customers need solutions for. The most successful businesses I have seen are anchored around this theme and fill in the details around it.

Businesses built for the long term will focus on creating the greatest customer value. These companies have developed a comprehensive solution that can meet a number of needs within that problem set. While custom problems can be solved, these companies have developed a solution that can also address unanticipated problems that might normally appear in similar situations. The broader the solution you can create, the more customers can come to you.

The challenge for the entrepreneur is to manage that process so solutions don't go so far down one path as to be unusable in other environments. My business plan has always been to create a flexible product that answers many needs and solves many problems, even if it takes a little longer to build and costs a little more. What my company has done is create a solution and product that appeals to a broader audience and gives me more flexibility in meeting changing market demands.

Determine and Maintain Your Focus

One of the challenges I faced early in my entrepreneurial career was deciding what type of business I was in: Was I a consultant/services provider, or was I making a product? The mindset for running a pure services organization is completely different from that for running a product company. While both are devoted to providing solutions to customers' problems, the consulting organization is focused on building an organization with proven methodologies for solving similar problems. In a leadership role, you have to focus on ensuring that your company remains centered on this area of expertise, since your customers will come to you because of your reputation for solving these particular issues. Customers also pay you for services as you provide them, so you have fewer up-front expenses, and your cash flow depends on the time it takes to complete an engagement. As the manager, you will also be very focused on developing new customers and selling your services.

Product companies are also focused on solving customer problems, but their answers are developed in a completely different manner. Product companies do attempt to develop standardized solutions for solving similar types of problems, but there is much more risk involved. While consultants get paid as they go along, product companies develop products they hope to get paid for in the future. If you're making a product, you have to invest in research and development and a sales force to generate customers. You must create a support organization to assist your customers and ensure the product is performing as you said it would.

17

Obviously, for a product company, there is increased risk and an increased need for investment. Creating the first product and getting customers are formidable challenges, but executives must also look to the future. Product companies have to continuously enhance, particularly in the software industry. With computer hardware or other durable goods, once a product is completed, engineers and the company move onto another product or a next generation. Software has a more fluid business structure. Software developers must constantly enhance and improve because a product is really never "done." Software makers have to incorporate new technologies and make software usable in emerging environments. Software companies also have to design solutions that customers can easily integrate with existing legacy systems.

We did not make the decision to become a product company overnight. For almost six years our business was 50 percent consulting and 50 percent software product development. During that time, we were simultaneously working on two parallel paths – developing customized solutions for our customers' particular problems and seeking to create a standard solution that would solve the majority of the problems our customers were encountering.

There came a time when I realized the greater potential existed in developing the product rather than in performing the services. I saw that the market for software was changing and that standardized products would be essential for companies seeking to solve expensive problems in a short period of time. While businesses would still need consulting services for choosing and deploying solutions, if we devoted more time and capital to strengthening our solutions, we would have the opportunity to gain a leadership position in a rapidly emerging marketplace.

That decision was a calculated risk, but I realized we had a great advantage compared to our competition: We had spent a considerable amount of time in our market and achieved a formidable level of expertise. If our product efforts did not develop as quickly as we hoped, we could return to consulting to provide capital. Fortunately, we had developed a tangible product that companies responded to, allowing us to remain focused on developing and improving that solution for a wider market and extending our business footprint.

Build the Business

Once we decided we were in the business of producing software, gaining market share and acceptance while producing a reliable and powerful product was our early business strategy. We constantly revisited our internal and external constituencies and solicited their perceptions on where the market was headed. By maintaining these open channels of communication, we were quickly able to re-assess our goals and address concerns before they reached a critical stage. In addition, these constant conversations kept us focused on our core business: providing software that solved the real-world problems of manufacturers. We never pretended we did anything beyond that, but we constantly looked for ways to do that better than anyone else.

Because we are a software company, building the business required us to constantly gauge what technological innovations were having an impact on our customers. As our business grew, the challenge was that no one knew which emerging operating platforms would become the industry standard. We relied on being compatible with our customers' hardware, and that hardware was going to change very significantly. We had to talk with our current and potential customers and gauge where they were putting their resources and then decide how we could maximize our opportunity. Fortunately, we chose to devote our efforts to a system that became accepted throughout manufacturing, but it just as easily could have gone the other way. For me, the difference is that we listened to our customers and looked for ways we could work with them in developing solutions they would be most likely to use.

With the advent of the Internet, we again turned to our customers and looked for ways we could work with them to take advantage of this powerful technology. While many companies made pie-in-the-sky promises about what they could do using the Internet, we realized our customers did not want to hear about visions and dreams; they wanted to see repetitive, demonstrated success. Again, we developed solutions we heard our customers needed, and we worked with them to ensure our improvements and innovations were useful and necessary, and not made only for the sake of adding a few bells and whistles.

Generate and Maintain Business Momentum

Momentum in business is an overstated term. There is no such thing as a rising straight line of profit and market penetration. At the granular level, running a business is full of constant starts and stops. If you magnify that line on the graph, you'll find it is not smooth, but made up of daily fluctuations. Your goal as an entrepreneur is to keep those small movements trending toward the positive, for then you will have growth and increased profitability. As a leader, your focus should be on maximizing the upturns while minimizing the downturns.

For the entrepreneurial leader, the most important aspect of gaining "momentum" is persistence. In every stage of the business cycle, you will be challenged to respond to new situations and to manage conflicting internal constituencies. Moving our business forward requires me to keep focused on the landscape beyond the challenges directly in front of me.

Think of building momentum as taking your dog for a walk. You have a known path you want to walk, but the dog does not know that path. As you walk, the dog constantly goes out of his way to explore the areas outside the path. Your role is to keep the dog coming back to the main path. Sometimes the dog will find something interesting that requires more time to investigate, but more often he'll be looking around just to look around. Your ability to listen and respond to the needs of the dog, while simultaneously keeping the walk moving forward, demonstrates your persistence to the dog. Eventually, the dog realizes you are pulling him back onto the path only because there are new and better things to see, and the dog becomes much more interested in where you are going than where you are. Gaining momentum requires a firm hand on the leash, combined with a willingness to do some exploring as you go.

Carve Out a Niche

We have carved out our niche in the manufacturing industry through a constant commitment to customer service and consistent delivery of a reliable and secure product. Because we have been in the same industry for well over a decade, we can point to customers throughout a number of industries who have solved complex and expensive problems using our product. We have developed a staff whose expertise is unparalleled in our marketplace and made acquisitions to provide more enhanced levels of service. In everything we do, we focus on listening to our customers and solving their specific problems.

Build Your Team

Finding people for your management team starts with you. You have to look at your personal values and combine them with the values of your business. For me, I look for people who combine old-fashioned values – intelligence, honesty, integrity, hard work, and determination – with the problem-solving skills needed by our customers. Our company works with manufacturers, who as a group are very pragmatic and resistant to hype. I need people on our team to understand that our marketplace is not about sizzle and flash. Our customers look to us for the highest levels of reliability, because they are placing their entire manufacturing environments in our hands and depend on us to deliver. Many of the people I have interviewed recently are still looking for the Internet get-rich-quick scenario. That model will not work with our customers, and those folks would not be a good fit for our corporate vision. I need people who want to take the time to sit and listen to our customers, who want to engage and become involved, and who want to use technology to solve the customer's problem.

Another important aspect of finding people is making sure they are suited for the openings you have and how you expect to have that job done. Smaller entrepreneurial companies like ours have a very different way of doing things from large multinational corporations, and people coming out of that world are not really prepared for how much their job could change from day-to-day. Our environment is more attractive to people who like to take risks and are excited about the challenges and responsibilities that come from working in a small business. Unlike larger companies, where processes are sometimes as important as people, we attract team members from a wide variety of backgrounds who each bring new perspectives to our particular segment of the software industry. They come to us because they have a generalist perspective, a willingness to roll up their sleeves and learn new things. They do not hold a lot of preconceptions on how things should be done, and they want to develop the best way for our company to do things.

The longer people remain with you as your business grows, the more your staff will develop a corporate personality. The difficult challenge in expanding your staff is meshing the "old guard" with the new ideas being brought in. As the leader, you cannot be too married to old business methods. The world is changing, and your business will have to change in some ways to take advantage of new opportunities. The most important aspect you can control is the rate of change within the business. When you see the chance to seize an opportunity, you will have to bring in people with new experiences and work with them to help shape new understandings and theories for your established employees. You always have to remember that everyone looks to you for the roadmap and vision of where the business should be heading, and that you must work with all of your team members to push them toward that destination.

Take Leadership

I think one of the key things for me in leading a business is communication. The CEO charts the course and looks beyond the next bend in the road. The company looks for you to provide the strategic vision of where the business should be heading and how the organization will prepare and execute in getting there. Communication is vital in this role because you must establish a clear and consistent message: What business are we in? Why are we doing it? What happens after that? The best-run businesses are those in which everyone knows the answers to these questions because every employee goes about their job to meet those expectations. Everyone is on the same page, pulling in the same direction and helping the business pick up the momentum we discussed earlier.

You must use a number of different methods in communicating to the business. Generally, I am not a rah-rah type of personality, but I know everyone wants to know what I am thinking and where I see us headed. I take every opportunity in company meetings, through e-mails, in company-wide letters, and in one-on-one discussions, to communicate our vision and goals. Also, I want people to feel they can approach me at any time, so I want to be seen and involved in daily projects. I do not want to be a CEO who sits off to the side and appears once a quarter. I believe I have more credibility by maintaining regular interaction throughout the business.

With the economic challenges we have recently faced, speaking to the company is more difficult but even more necessary. Part of your role as a leader is keeping the highs from getting too high and the lows from getting too low. For example, in a boom economy, I have to keep people focused on staying lean and ensuring we stay focused on the core business. Conversely, in tough times, I have to keep everyone positive and working toward getting the company prepared for the economic turnaround. In any economic circumstance the leader is focused on maintaining the company's strategic path and preserving the business advantages already gained.

I most admire those leaders who can maintain a consistency of vision and action throughout a tumultuous period. For me, the most successful leaders are those who clearly articulate a vision and goal for their business, and then keep pulling people in that direction. People do not like to be herded and pushed, but they will respond to persistent tugging. The good leader is one who makes their employees move on their own, without coercion or force, because they have communicated across the organization that benefits arise from moving and that everyone's best interests are fulfilled by meeting those challenges.

One Thing at a Time

For a long time, I have had an old proverb hanging in my office: "If you want to get a lot of things done, do one thing at a time." This statement summarizes how I view my role as CEO. There are too many issues occurring in your business at any one time for you to possibly know about all of them, much less participate in any meaningful way. I always recommend that people prioritize what is important for them to accomplish and then focus on getting each of those tasks completed. The more items that crop up on your plate, the less likely it is you will ever finish any of them.

A corollary of this proverb recently came up in one of our board meetings: "Making little progress on a broad front will not get you where you want to go." Focusing resources on accomplishing critical tasks is an absolute business imperative for any CEO. You are the only person who can direct the company and its energy towards achieving one or two critical goals that will make the difference. You must always be aware of where the majority of your resources, both personal and company-wide, are being directed, and you must ensure that the goals are being met before the time and resources are lost.

Dave Cone leads Camstar in its mission to deliver world-class collaborative manufacturing solutions. Mr. Cone has worked in the manufacturing industry for more than 20 years. Before founding Camstar, he worked for IBM, where he was a West Coast manufacturing systems consultant responsible for the implementation of manufacturing resource planning (MRP) systems.

In 1984 Mr. Cone founded Camstar and has since grown the company into a global software company. He holds a BS in mathematics from the University of North Carolina at Chapel Hill, an MS in operations research from Stanford, and an MBA from the University of California, Berkeley.

WEALTH WITHOUT GUILT: FOUNDING A BUSINESS ON PRINCIPLES

STEVE DEMOS
White Wave
Founder and President

Getting the Business Off the Ground

Getting started was not easy for White Wave, but it never is for anybody. It takes a lot of sweat equity and learning, no matter what kind of business you happen to be in. At the start of any venture, you have to accept that there will be failures, lots of failures, and you have to believe you will overcome them.

When we began manufacturing tofu, we had more obstacles than most. First, we were planning to make and sell soy, a product universally disliked. Second, there was no product category, no industry, and virtually no customers. Beyond that, we had no background in business. And yet we felt there was a place for a company that would fundamentally change the basic business model. We weren't sure how we were going to do it, but our goal was to build a successful company based on the following ideals: We would make products that were healthy, and with which we would do no harm to humanity or to the planet. It was a simple, elegant idea that would prove extremely difficult to realize. I suppose that's what makes our ultimate success so gratifying.

When we started White Wave in Boulder, Colorado, in the late 1970s, our first task was to introduce tofu to the grocery trade. But since this had never been done before with any kind of success, we were faced with selling a product that was completely unproven. The only place soy had been successful was within the Oriental community. But even there, tofu sold well only around the Chinese New Year, and not very well at other times. The odds were not in our favor.

For us to get access to grocery stores, we had to prove the product had a following and that it would do well enough to warrant shelf space. Of course, as I just noted, there was no following.

To make matters worse, our packaging was primitive. We had the tofu in a plastic bag in a Chinese carry out carton – it looked like the little bag in which you carry goldfish home from the county fair. The first grocery store manager we approached almost died in hysterical laughter when I presented such an item. It was so basic and so terribly marketed.

Once we repackaged the product, we went back to that first grocery store, and the manager said, "I'll give you two stores. Come back in 30 days, and we will evaluate the movement to determine whether there has been enough to warrant putting you on the shelves in other stores."

We were not confident that the products would sell, so we had our employees actually go out and buy our own product. Every day, they would buy tofu off the shelves. In doing so, they created the impression that there was a consumer out there buying. We went back for the evaluation 30 days later, and the supermarket was very impressed. We got the supermarket chain.

So our first traction was created with consumer support, smoke, and mirrors. When starting a business, you have to be persistent and creative to get things done.

Landing Those First Clients

Our tofu was largely sold only in health food stores for several years, but we always had the ambition of reaching mainstream America with our products. The problem was that we were manufacturing a product that we liked, but that most average Americans considered distasteful, and that they didn't know how to use.

In response, we developed Silk soymilk in the mid-1990s. Unlike traditional soymilk, which tasted "beany," Silk was packaged in square boxes and sold warm. We developed flavorful soymilk, packaged it in familiar "milk" cartons, and marketed it to be sold cold in the dairy case. The product would be familiar to consumers and would taste good, and people would know how to use it – just like milk.

But like tofu many years earlier, we first had to gain entry into the marketplace. It was critical in the launch of Silk that we were on as many shelves as possible because it was a perishable food. We estimated that we had to get on several hundred shelves all in the same week.

To do so, I went on the road – I called this road trip the Silk Parade. I think I traveled 40,000 miles, flying around the country presenting this product, but even so, that only got me into a third of the stores we needed to be in. So we developed a virtual sales presentation, a breakfast we mailed to supermarket buyers. We used Fiesta serving ware and included spoons, cloth napkins, cereal, Silk, berries, and granola. We also added a rose in a water stem and a copy of the *Boulder Psychic Times*. For every buyer we sent that to, we placed product the week that we needed to. We were batting a thousand on the concept, and that is how we actually launched the Silk product into most of the trade.

Entrepreneurial Momentum Won't Happen Overnight

As you can tell from our beginning, building momentum was difficult. It took more than 18 years of making and selling different types of soy products to reach where we wanted to be. If you want to increase your business momentum, you must be patient, determined, and resourceful. You also must be willing to increase anxiety, stress, and risk in your life. Ironically, with all that will come an underpinning of confidence as you move forward. You can't just step out into the unknown and then continue dialing it up without some return on your risk. There is no question that the anxiety, stress, and risk factors go up as you build a business, but you will feel, even though it may seem to be a contradiction, that you are on firmer footing.

Why is that? I think it's because once some of your risks start to pay off, you'll have a track record of proving that whatever you're thinking is doable. If you continue to maintain an accurate forecasting of the next fundamental momentum step, then you are constantly verifying to yourself, "I'm on target, I'm on target."

The lesson we learned is that you must keep taking risks – even if it takes years. Not many get-rich-quick schemes work. Most are get-rich-slow schemes.

Business Techniques to Avoid

Since we founded White Wave on a business model that remained true to our vision of not causing harm, we worked hard to never compromise. In the business world, however, this is difficult to accomplish, and we discovered a number of good lessons along the way.

One of the most important lessons I learned is to avoid the urge to out-think the customer and the market. Together, they are your partners. If you are shrewd to the point of being exploitative, this stratagem will only boomerang on you: You won't get the credibility you are looking for or the repeat customers you want. We once had a person working for us who knew more about the flow of our product through the business chain than anyone else in the company, and who made more money for the company than anyone else. This man was so bright that he could out-think the other side and often did. But eventually, his ability came back to haunt him and us. I discovered we were making more money off our customers than we said we would. This fellow had out-thought the customer, and even though it enhanced the profitability of White Wave, I thought it would be fundamentally destructive to the company, so we parted ways.

It is important to stay true to your ideals and to constantly strive to maintain the focus on what you believe and why you're in business. You may not always succeed in that pursuit, but the more you are able to stay on the path, the more your business will benefit.

Getting the Right People to Join the Team

If you want to find the right people, you have to stand for something. As I've mentioned, at White Wave we stand for some pretty strong ideals. Whatever you believe in as a company, you have to make sure the people you hire understand what that is. Otherwise, you're fishing – out there looking for bodies to fill positions. You should be looking for compatibility on the philosophical level, as well as on a work-ethic level. Then, you have to listen to your intuition very carefully because no matter how smart the person looks, no matter how dazzling the résumé may be, no matter what mega corporation they were with or what mega success they may have had, it's irrelevant to your business. It's relevant only that they bring a work experience that enhances their skills. I think the easiest thing to do when you're young and looking for talent is to be dazzled by résumés and credentials.

We've hired people with dazzling résumés, and more often than not, they fail. In fact, I would give our success rate in very highly credentialed résumés a seven out of 10 failure rate. That may surprise people, but it's true. Because of this, regardless of résumé, we've developed the ability to decide within a short time in an interview whether a person will work or not. Within seconds of walking into an interview, I just know. I can't quantify or tell you exactly why, but it's not just me – others at

White Wave have this skill, as well. Perhaps it's because we have such a clearly defined vision of what we stand for, and it's easy to tell when someone doesn't fit. I've learned to listen to my gut. When you go contrary to your instinct, it costs you more; it can cause great political and personal disruption in the company, as well as corporate damage associated with separating somebody from the company. That's far more difficult than holding off on hiring and carrying the work load for a little longer.

Management Style – You Have to Have Vision

I suppose I consider myself a dictator in management style, but one I hope who listens to and solicits intelligent, creative, and forward-thinking input, as well as encourages people to make mistakes, because that implies that a person is taking action. I also encourage people to learn from their mistakes so that we move forward. I try to surround myself with people who are better than I am in particular areas. At first, an entrepreneur is required to do 10 jobs they never dreamed of doing, but eventually, if the business is going to expand, you have to relinquish some of the things you've done on your own to people who are skilled in particular areas.

I'm not, however, big on consensus decision-making because that often implies the lowest common denominator and lacks creative thought. Of course, if your entire management team thinks your idea is crazy, you should reflect seriously on it. But even so, it does not mean I won't go ahead and take action on my own. I have – though not often – gone against the stream internally and have prevailed. That is what I get paid to do, and it's why I think I've had success. Being an entrepreneur is not for the faint of heart. Often the future isn't as clear to someone else as it may be to you. You have to have confidence in your own vision if you're going to be an effective leader.

In a Turbulent Economy, Stress Fundamentals

When times turn downward, you have to focus on fundamentals. Make sure the money-making part of your business model is intact and that you invest in it. If your model is a service, then it's at the serviceperson's level; if you manufacture a product, it's at the product level; if you generate ideas, it's at the idea level. You fundamentally have to protect the gold mine. If, because of the economy, you're no longer able to enhance your performance by volume, you have to enhance your performance at the moneymaking level. In manufacturing, instead of growing the category, you must grow the gross margin. Once the downturn ends – and sooner or later they always end – then you're well prepared to attack the market.

In terms of making money during a recession, it's a fallacy to think you can't make money while the economy as a whole suffers. In fact, you should be able to make more money in a down economy than in an up economy. During down times, you increase your war chest and just bask in dropping it all to the bottom line.

It's Not Bad to be Small

When you're relatively small, you can turn on a dime, as White Wave has proved, compared to the large food and beverage conglomerates that are among our competitors. We create and innovate, and they don't. Everyone at White Wave is empowered to respond to and act on market circumstances, without having to cover their butt because they are trying to climb the corporate ladder. They can make mistakes in our environment and not be punished on a career level. And that means we can change very fast.

Another advantage of being small is that we don't have as much capital invested, so we can change the basic way we manufacture something. When we introduced Silk, it was my analysis that there was an $80 million market out there that we would be attacking. All of the other manufacturers had financed their factories around the packaging system of traditional soymilk in aseptic boxes, which were sold warm next to soup on the store shelves. The large companies would never change that until we hurt them. They wouldn't change because they had a debt service. That means they were risk-averse to changing where the product was placed in the supermarket. Until they saw that someone was beating them, they weren't going to risk not paying the bank. As a result of that, we figured we had two years before anyone would figure out we were hurting them. We were wrong. It took them five years.

That was a critical mistake on their part. If they had reacted inside two years, we would probably be in a much more evenly divided market. As it is, Silk controls 80 percent of the market, far more than we expected in the marketplace. A mega-corporation is more deeply and more strategically committed to a certain course, and if you identify a mispositioned product or a miscalculated procedure from a manufacturer, then the big company is usually not sharp enough to drop their current momentum and invest in a risk momentum the way a smaller and hungrier company can.

Carving out a Niche in the Marketplace

If you plan to differentiate yourself from the competition, make sure your product has clear, valuable differentiations. A clear, valuable differentiation may be that you make the cheapest stuff on the market. It might be a piece of garbage, but it's the lowest-priced product. It could be that you make the most expensive piece on the market, but it is of greater value for the dollar spent than the competition. The key point here is differentiate, differentiate, differentiate. And be authentic: Your product still needs to have authenticity as a benefit. The consumer should be buying not only the perception of a benefit, but the actual derived benefit. If you attempt to sell something that's not there, it eventually will catch up to you. If you can give them the net effect of benefit, then you have a niche product. You've created something that people are not getting anywhere else, and that creates brand loyalty.

Big Companies as Partners – Know Them Well

When you make soy, you have two strikes against you with a fastball flying right at you. When we started, soy was one of the most hated foods in the country. In fact, during the early 1980s, the *Los Angeles Times* ranked soy as the second worst food, right behind liver. Nobody believed the product would succeed. When one of our first bankers asked me what I did for a living, and I told him I made tofu, his whole demeanor became apologetic – as if that was the saddest thing he'd ever heard.

So how did we build credibility and support from the corporate players with whom we needed to work? We needed to work with large manufacturers to produce our products. We did not have our own soymilk facilities, but some manufacturers were hesitant to deal with a small, unproven company. So I made sure I understood how they made money, and then I designed my approach to them that explained how White Wave would make them more money than their average client. I said, for instance, "Listen, I know the pricing range, and I know you'll make a premium amount on me, because I want to be in your factory and prove to you that we not only bring value to your factory but we bring ease of manufacturing, too. And when I've proven this, I'll come back and ask you to split that with me."

We basically have built into our negotiations and pricing strategy a future benefit to manufacturing facilities that isn't evident when we start up – and it has always worked.

Plan Your Work, Work Your Plan

There's a saying in scuba diving: Plan your dive, dive your plan. I have adapted that for business: Plan your work, work your plan. There are two important pieces here: One is to realistically and accurately envision a forecast that you know you can live with but that still challenges the people to do more than they are doing today. Once that is in place, you have to measure how you're doing. Within any organization, you have to have a system that measures your constant progress toward the goal you have identified. You measure what we call "plan to actual." I don't think there is anything ingenious about this; it's just the discipline of planning properly, getting everybody in the plan, and then getting everybody reporting back so you know how you're doing.

In working our plan, we build in a process in which we empower our executives and middle management to take control. The budgetary allocation process has a wonderful empowerment system built into it, though as a leader, it's my job to make sure all of our numbers add up to 100. I also have to make sure I have chosen the right people and they know the strategy of the day and our priorities. I verify this by seeing that they are heading in the right direction and making good decisions. As long as it's strategically in sync with where I am trying to guide the company, then I don't tell them how to do it or why to do it.

Even so, a leader plays a crucial role to ensure his or her company executes. As an example, I change approximately 30 percent to 40 percent of all budgets during the course of a year because people can get off target. In other words, I don't empower people with a "Here's the budget, do anything you want" approach. I take the responsibility of saying, "No, you're off target there." That can be really tough, because you have to do it diplomatically so that you don't demoralize people or neuter the empowerment you're trying to support. That's the fine line between being autocratic and truly being a leader. For each entrepreneur, I think that's a learning process.

With me, and I suspect many entrepreneurs who have had success, it is difficult to always allow people to exercise power, because as a leader, you know what you want done. And you've learned to rely on your intuition in building a company. It's a constant balancing act.

In addition, I find that I treat people based on how they've performed in the past. If someone has an idea that will cost a million dollars, I say come back to me with exact costs and timing for when I'll see a difference. That person then has to quantify all of that, and I'll measure how they've done. The next time he or she comes back and asks me for $10 million, I'll look at what they did the last time. Every time someone rings the bell, I'll give them more until they prove me wrong or themselves wrong. The people who have risen in the company to have the most power are those who have consistently delivered results.

Be an Example for Employees

If you expect your employees to follow your vision, you better make sure you live it. Make sure you're authentic. You have to be careful that you are constantly measuring your own actions against what you want people to believe. If you deviate, acknowledge it and come back to base. I believe in the power of being right – when you're right, you're right, and everybody knows it and everybody climbs on when they smell something that's right. In addition to leading the company from a business perspective, it's also my job to make sure that from all sides I'm exuding authenticity. I must live what I preach.

But, like everyone else, I'm not perfect. When you have a clear, concise vision of a company, as you should, it's often tough to live up to. I'm willing to acknowledge that I make plenty of mistakes. If you hit the ball three out of 10 times in baseball, they'll put you in the Hall of Fame. I'm sure I'm making at least those seven mistakes out there, but the key is I'll acknowledge that and tell employees I was wrong. I think people like to know you're imperfect and you're willing to move forward.

Thriving on Change in the Marketplace

We live and breathe change at White Wave. Half of the people we employ are here to help initiate change, and the guy at the top never stops tweaking and changing things in the model. However, at the same time we encourage change, we also strive to have a disciplined company that is measurable, predictable, and controllable with systems that are repetitive. This may seem a contradiction, but it is not. Both change and consistency are important. If you, an employee, can justify to me that a certain change will improve the overall operations, we'll support you. In short, we strive for change, but only if you come up with something that is compatible with the vision, strategy, and ethos of the company. Of course, that implies that we have been effective in communicating the ethos and strategy to the employees and are not operating so far out in left field that they lose direction. It's incumbent on us to ensure that we inspire in the right direction.

Success Is Not Measured by Money Alone

Though there are traditional measurements of success, I measure it by how close I have come to my original mission. It's looking at my ability to envision accurately, and then to produce and deliver something that improves upon where I started. Now, if you're fortunate enough to be a very good businessperson, you make lots of money. And, if you're fortunate enough to be a good leader and a cultural designer, then you get to be a good guy at the top. There are other factors of appraising success, and you don't have to have all of them to be considered successful.

I don't care if people like me; I do care if they respect me, because that means I'm authentic in my principles. I don't care if we make money, but I couldn't be in business if we didn't. And I really don't care if I make people rich doing it, but what a great business model if we're true to our vision and everyone else gets rich, too.

In building this business model – I call it "wealth without guilt" – I'm not trying to teach anybody but myself. If people are inspired to follow our lead, though, that's great. I started White Wave because I couldn't find a business model I wanted to join as an employee. That doesn't mean there are not many good models out there, but I couldn't find one I really wanted to believe in. So I said, "What a wonderful thing if I could have a career proving to myself something that I intuitively understood – that I can be good to the planet and good to humanity and still do very well monetarily." I'm not doing anything differently than any other businessperson is doing. I'm just making very select, conscious choices at a fundamental level early in the game, so I don't have to compromise later on. I didn't want to make products that hurt people. Soy was strictly the vehicle for that business model. It could have been anything. It's just that I couldn't find anything else I believed in that was compatible to the concept of soy. But that was more of personal preference. Other people have made wonderful contributions in the medical field or scientific research.

I think if you have a vision and a passion, your business and life become that much easier. You're work isn't just about money. It's about something you really believe in, and it's much easier working 18-hour days when that is the case.

The Importance of Customer Service

There is only one definition of a business. I don't care what you have; I don't care what service you provide. It has nothing to do with the product; it has to do with having a customer. The day you have one customer, you have a business. If I sell you my old leaves in the fall from my yard, I have a leaf business. I don't care what the particulars are. If that's the core definition of the business, then there is no limit to what you should do in protecting your customer. If you were to look at the cost you incurred to get that customer, you'd be astounded by it and what your retrieval cost might be. In some cases we've had imperfect product and imperfect circumstances, and we've lost customers. There was nothing I could do about it, because at the time I didn't have a solution to my problem. I would have to accept that loss as part of the process of growing a company. But in getting back and keeping customers, we've always tried to make the customer feel like an individual we care about, not a number or a homogenous part of society. The more you individualize customer service, the more that customer will brag about you and become an enthusiast of your brand.

Bringing Vision to Your Business

What makes a great leader? Vision. Real vision. I don't believe we have leaders in this country right now. We have people who are making a living from taking the lowest common denominator of opinion and voicing that to the masses because democracy tends to promote non-visionary leadership. In business it is sometimes the reverse, because business is not a democracy. You're rewarded for coming up with a great vision. Even so, there aren't very many leaders because we are in an environment that is not conducive to that goal.

The greatest example that we are not making leaders is that in many companies, the CFO winds up becoming the CEO. That's not because of vision; that's mechanical execution in management. They are called the leader, but what are they leading? They are leading disciplines. I understand that, but they are not envisioning change and forward improvement.

The upshot here is that to be an effective entrepreneur, you must lay out a vision and then inspire your company to passionately pursue it. If you believe in it, don't allow anything to move you from your goal.

Be Innovative, Different; Be Good Stewards of Society

In a mature culture and mature society, it's getting harder and harder to enter the business stream unless you do so with real innovation. The vast majority of entrepreneurial ventures will come out of scientific or technological innovations because they are different, unique, and easier to chase and establish funding for – for example, making a new soda to compete against Pepsi and Coke. There will also be a rise of support for businesses that deliver product comparable to what exists today but with superior corporate ethos, because they stand for something more than the big conglomerates do. Both of those strategies will be an opportunity for entrepreneurial momentum because we will have limited resources, lots of choices, and lots of people having to decide among products that are virtually the same. To answer their dilemma, what a company stands for will go a long way.

If you can do both, you will have a distinct advantage over the competition. As we've learned over the past 25 years, work hard, take risks, be patient, and believe in what you're setting out to accomplish.

As founder and president of White Wave, Steve Demos is responsible for the strategic direction and all operations of the company. In 1977, after traveling through India and other parts of the East for three years, and spending eight weeks meditating in California, Mr. Demos founded White Wave. He began by making tofu in a bucket and delivering it to local stores in a little red wagon. His entrepreneurial spirit paid off, and he has been running White Wave ever since.

Mr. Demos earned a bachelor's degree in American studies from Bowling Green University.

ENTREPRENEURSHIP 101: FROM VALIDATION TO VIABILITY

MIKE TURNER

Waveset Technologies

Chief Executive Officer and Founder

Building Validation

As an entrepreneur, you gain unique insights into the viability of a startup. To start, you must determine whether an idea provides a lucrative investment opportunity. Determining whether an idea is worth investment is based on three basic principles:

1. Does it confront a pervasive problem?
2. Is the problem urgent?
3. Is this a problem people are willing to spend money to solve?

These are the willingness to pay, urgent problem, and pervasive problem principles. If any of these principles are imbalanced, the business will face significant challenges in building and sustaining momentum. To ensure against this, entrepreneurs should employ a process of due diligence supported by in-depth research and market validation. The process of market validation requires:

1. A defined target audience
2. A strong understanding of the target market's business drivers
3. A series of value propositions that address unique and specific needs
4. A sophisticated survey tool
5. A disciplined methodology for unbiased consideration and evaluation of the research data

Only after investing the time and resources to validate a market opportunity is the entrepreneur ready to move to the next step, that of courting and securing funding.

Three Phases of Early-Stage Companies

The secret of venture capitalism's relationship to the market is that there are no billion-dollar niches. Smart investors look for $100-$150 million markets that meet an underserved need. Startups that succeed in leveraging these opportunities focus on a narrow, solvable problem and are driven by an experienced management team. The key is to get to market as quickly as possible, verify your position in the market, and ultimately translate that "niche" success into success in other areas.

When building a business plan, an entrepreneur must establish a strong financial strategy that demonstrates fiscal responsibility and a forward-looking ability to achieve profitability. In the high-tech world, initial funding is usually secured from venture capital firms, which typically define investment rounds in terms of Series A, B, and C. Series A is primarily used to fund research and development efforts, with the goal of bringing a viable product to market for "mass" consumption. If a product is well-received and establishes traction in its target market, then the deal generally progresses to Series B. Series B is focused on building a repeatable – or scalable – sales model. At this stage, revenue matters primarily as a means of facilitating further product development and the services necessary to support it. Success achieved in Series B naturally leads to Series C. In

Series C, the methodology applied in Series B is leveraged on a broader scale – nationally and internationally – with an eye toward profitability. At this stage, the goal is to grow market share and establish the company as one to be reckoned with among its competitors.

For early-stage startups, reaping a profit from early customers is less important than winning client loyalty and ensuring customer satisfaction. In contrast, companies preparing to go public have to worry about the profit and loss ratios associated with an ever-looming bottom line.

Psychological Drivers of Corporate Spending

Economic behavior tends to waver between extreme optimism and extreme pessimism, and entrepreneurs must run their businesses accordingly. In an optimistic economy people are focused on top-line revenue growth. They will do anything they can to enlarge the pie, and they rarely worry about downside risks or cost concerns. Investors invest readily; end-users consume enthusiastically; and all boats lift with the rising tide.

In a pessimistic economy people are concerned with issues of cost, risk, and optimization. As a result, businesses tend to focus inwardly and manage their operations conservatively. Investors invest more warily; end-users consume more selectively; and in the end, only the strong survive.

Entrepreneurs must be acutely aware of revolving economic cycles and their effects on the current business climate. Momentum tends to shift often and dramatically, and when leveraged intelligently, can carry a smart company to success through unlikely ups and downs.

Startup Advantages

Historically, there has never been a better time in the history of the world to start a business. Information in the Internet Age is readily accessible and travels at the speed of light, literally. As a result, people are better connected and better informed. This ubiquity of technology – increasingly standardized and applied to all walks of life – has driven the interdependence of global markets, providing infinite opportunities for entrepreneurs with vision. A key factor in leveraging these opportunities is flexibility.

Flexibility is the greatest advantage a startup has over larger, more well-established companies. Startups can change strategic direction almost instantaneously. More important, they can *truly* focus on making their customers happy, regardless of their needs. A smart startup will do whatever it takes to help its customers succeed – in essence, aligning its budget with its customers' needs. In contrast, large companies are limited by the size and bureaucratic complexity of their organizations, a fact that handicaps their ability to provide customized service to a broad and often highly diverse client base.

Where possible, the first few clients of a startup should be secured through prior business relationships. It is customary for highly individualized, discounted deals to be offered to these customers, who ultimately become a company's first – and most important – competitive references. Larger companies can rarely compete with these deals because of revenue constraints. As a result, what a larger company might view as a losing deal is often a great deal for a startup. This is another example of how a younger, more nimble company can outmaneuver its larger, slower competitors.

It's About the People

The ability to build the right team depends on your network and how well that network leverages other trusted resources. If a company is venture-backed, its investment firm has a vested interest in seeing it build a strong, seasoned management team and will often suggest candidates for senior-level positions.

There is, however, something to be said for known quantities. If an individual has a proven track record that is validated by others in your organization, then bring him on-board; if he is an unknown entity, then take the time and resources to evaluate him carefully. One of the best ways to do this is through "back channel" references – contacts he did not provide, but who offer particularly insightful and specific commentary, nonetheless. In today's high-tech world, a business is only as good as its people; never hire an unknown person without strong back-channel references!

A Company Has a Culture – One Way or Another

The culture is the personality of the company. Every company has a personality that either is created or evolves by itself. One way to drive culture "creation" is to reward and motivate people when they exhibit desired behaviors. Incentive programs should validate and reinforce the corporate culture based on the mission and vision of the organization. Alternatives can range from increased equity awards or salary increases to providing special opportunities for peer-to-peer and executive-to-team member recognition. One example of a unique, highly successful award is the C2 – or Conserve Capital – award, given to an individual who does something extraordinary to save the company money. The award instills pride in its recipient and encourages others to do the same.

A positive work environment fosters a strong team with an undivided spirit. It is much easier for a company to build and sustain momentum when it works well together, than when it doesn't. The company vision should serve to unify employees. It should be easily understood and well-defined as to how it will be achieved. And everyone should understand his or her role in making it happen. Often in a startup, there is no time to train people to do their jobs. Individuals need to be highly motivated – able to learn on the fly and work independently, with little or no direction. At the same time, they need to be strong team players whose particular actions correspond to the collective flow and direction of the company.

A key skill of a successful entrepreneur is to translate this energy into positive momentum and convince all his constituents – investors, analysts, partners, customers, and employees – that he can keep it on his side. Ultimately, momentum is psychological, and when people feel stalled or frustrated, they are less likely to see the forest for the trees. Success depends on an extraordinary group of humans working together to achieve an extraordinary set of goals. If a team believes the goals are unrealistic – and therefore unachievable – it's likely they will apply themselves only half-heartedly, consuming valuable time and resources, but delivering little or no resulting impact. As an entrepreneur, it's incumbent upon you to inspire your team's best work by providing "stretch" goals that build confidence and instill pride in an organization. You must do this by demonstrating how each individual's contribution – whether it's in sales, marketing, or product development – supports the overall mission and vision of the company, driving value and perpetual energy into the business.

CEO Responsibilities

In establishing a business, the CEO of a startup has to build a team that he trusts to manage the day-to-day operational responsibilities of the company. The CEO should focus on vision, while his team focuses on execution. To maintain the connection between vision and execution, management issues should be prioritized as either urgent or important. Urgent issues create unnecessary distractions, and while important, they should not get in the way of important issues, which define the long-term goals for success.

For example, an important issue for a startup is fiscal management. In a startup, a dollar spent is a dollar withdrawn from the collective pocket. The goal is to be intelligently frugal, but not cheap. A CEO must take good care of his employees by investing money where it needs to be spent, which in the early stages is primarily in research and development. Then, as the company grows and adopts an increasingly external focus, a transition should take place in which investment expands to support broader initiatives across areas such as marketing and business development.

Another responsibility of a CEO is to focus on the talent of his personnel. The CEO must genuinely show he cares as much about each individual's role in the company – their career goals and ambitions – as he does for the company as a whole. This also means the CEO must believe in the abilities of his "assistant coaches" to do their jobs better than he can himself. He must assume the team he has assembled is the best at what they do, worrying only to the extent that they have the resources and commitment they need to execute their jobs according to the vision of the company.

Here is something to keep in mind: Sometimes a CEO can overdrive an organization. In fact, what may take an hour or less to decide – and get passed down as a directive – may take a week or more to accomplish as it processes through an organization. In sum, CEOs need to be good at managing their own expectations.

As a CEO, there is tremendous pressure to push the ball as fast as possible, but the employees run the patterns.

To sustain a vision requires a clear and deliberate definition of goals. A CEO should identify corporate-wide goals on a quarterly basis, with the intent of increasing the value and momentum of his organization. And each team needs to have a meaningful set of goals that contribute to this value creation – for employees, partners, customers, and shareholders alike. The bottom line is all about building a successful, valuable company. This takes the efforts of numerous talented individuals working together toward a common goal – and it all starts with the CEO: his ability to identify the vision, set the direction, and then get out of the way and let his team run for the finish!

Mike Turner, CEO and founder of Waveset Technologies, Inc., brings 16 years of industry experience in building and growing successful companies. Most recently he served as entrepreneur-in-residence at AV Labs. He joined AV Labs from Tivoli Systems Inc., where he was vice president and general manager of its $1.2 billion enterprise business unit.

In 1996 Mr. Turner spearheaded the company's entry into the enterprise security space, resulting in revenue growth from $0 to $200 million in just two years. Mr. Turner's proven ability to turn business strategies into tangible market results contributed to significant successes at Convex Corporation and Tivoli Systems Inc., which he helped grow from a startup to a $1.8 billion industry leader in less than 10 years.

NAVIGATING YOUR ENTREPRENEURSHIP THROUGH CHOPPY STARTUP WATERS

FREDERICK A. BEER
Auragen Communications
Cofounder, President, and Chief Executive Officer

What's Your Core Difference?

Being an entrepreneur is like being captain of your own ship. You must know what port you are sailing for; you must chart your course; you must lead your crew; and you must handle course changes and difficulties along the way. You need to solve problems and get results. You must move quickly and decide your company's fate.

To accomplish all of this you need a guide. Here are some thoughts to help guide you through the often treacherous waters on the way to entrepreneurship: a clear passionate direction, a great culture, clarity on your market opportunity, and well-executed operations.

Your Direction

You cannot be everything to everyone. To try to be is to fail. You must focus on your core competencies. Your direction must eliminate options. It must bring clarity to you and your staff about strategies and actions that will be taken. It must dictate which opportunities you will take advantage of and those you won't. Focusing makes decisions and actions easier. At each decision point, you ask, "Does this match where I am headed?" If it does, you do it. If it doesn't, you don't. The challenge is sticking to this direction when things get tough. You must stay true to your direction or consciously change it.

Often what I call a company's direction is referred to as the vision and mission. The problem I have with these words is that they are used inconsistently – different companies and books use them in different contexts. Rather than get caught up in the appropriate label, the import thing is to have clarity and be passionate regarding where you are headed. You need to be able to imagine the future and how your company fits into it. This doesn't need to be crystal clear (it can't be, by definition, since you are looking at the future), but it does need to provide clarity as to the decisions and actions you will take. It needs to limit options to focus efforts and, ironically, create more options. If you focus on a few key items and do those better than anyone else you will be successful.

The most important characteristic of your direction is to do what you love – follow your passion and have a desire to make your imagined future a reality. To be successful you have to be able to sell your direction, to separate problems from solutions, to understand your own strengths and weaknesses, and to listen very carefully to what employees are saying and what the market is telling you. There is a lot of responsibility on your shoulders, but if you really love what you are doing, bumps in the road present themselves as opportunities or challenges, rather than problems. If you are really focused on where you are going, you won't be distracted by the inevitable detours.

Having a compelling picture of the future leads to taking action to make this picture a reality. After you have recognized an opportunity, research and data analysis can determine whether a market exists and whether you can make a profit with a given business model. From that point, you have to crystallize your direction into something that can be communicated. You have to trust your gut and follow your passion. This direction needs to be evangelized among employees, partners, investors, and customers. Your stakeholders need to buy into your direction. When they are committed to your direction, you will find them taking action without your oversight. A common passionate direction can be a terrific way to empower people – to set them loose.

A great way to accomplish this buy-in is, after you have become clear yourself, to gather input from others and gradually expand the circle of feedback until all stakeholders are involved. In the end, it takes a lot longer to create a direction this way, but there is an enormous amount of buy-in because people have felt their voices have been heard. You don't need to accept everyone's feedback, but it is important to listen to all of it and demonstrate to them that you have heard what they have to say.

Your Culture

A culture is a key component of any successful business. Often in a startup the excitement and passion about creating the business create a successful culture. This isn't a permanent culture, though, since it is predicated on items that can change quickly when growth slows or unexpected storms appear. Values can help propel this excitement and passion beyond those initial stages.

The foundation of a corporate culture comes from setting values that employees "live." You must start by defining values that you, as the entrepreneur, believe in. This isn't a simple task. Let's take honesty as an example – one of my company's values. At first glance it seems to be a relatively innocent and easy value to live up to. But when you dig more deeply, you need to really think about whether you can live this value in tough times. You must ask such questions as: "If I have a $100,000 deal on the line and I can sign the deal by being dishonest, would I?" To be successful, your values need to be deeply held ideals. A good question to ask is, "Would you follow your values if doing so meant losing your business?" You should be able to answer yes to this question.

Once you are clear on what you truly value, then you need to involve other employees. Remember you are creating values for your company, not just for yourself. It is important for you as the leader to personally live the values (which is why it is important to start with your values); you must also have employees live the company values. By involving others in the process of creating the values, you also establish an important aspect of your culture: "I respect your decisions and input."

Once your values are established, you must make sure they are lived. This starts with you, the leader, modeling the values every day. You should interview candidates with values in mind, communicate and develop stories about how the values have been lived and how they have benefited the company, and include values in orientations and reviews. When I review my management team, I interview many of their staff and ask, "Is your manager living our values?"

Values help instill a certain spirit that becomes the foundation of a corporate culture. The values at my company, Auragen Communications, are honesty and integrity, open communications, continuous improvement, and "Auragenality." These values have provided a foundation that is clear to every employee. Many companies publish their mission on a plaque, hang it in a conference room, and never mention it again. Publishing them on plaques can be an effective way of making people aware of them, but you cannot just publish them. You must follow through, making them a part of the company.

Your Market Opportunity

Of course, you have to produce something people want to buy. The trick is discovering what people are willing to pay for that they aren't buying now or that they aren't satisfied buying now. Once you have found a niche, it is important to build robust sales and marketing strength, particularly when things are going well. Sales and marketing is the lifeblood of every organization. You have to look at both the current market opportunity and the future market opportunity. Is the market growing or shrinking? What are your competitors doing? Is there a large corporation waiting for your niche to become big enough to interest them? These types of questions should be continually asked. Often success can lead to different competitors and different challenges. If you look out for these ahead of time, you will be better off.

What do customers want from your product or service? Think not only about what customers say they want, but also what they imply they want. Customers said they wanted a stylish car, but also convenience and space. The minivan initially contradicted the first in customers' minds but squarely reached other desires. In fact, early tests said the minivan would fail because it wasn't viewed as stylish. Don't let a single customer or a single want influence your view of the opportunity.

It is important to look at emotional elements customers want, as well. Do they want peace of mind, creativity, excitement, and fun? Customers for each product or service will desire different emotions to be stressed. Understanding what your market is looking for and what competitors are offering is very important. You must be able to differentiate your offering to customers. Differentiating beyond product features into emotional elements is very important for long-term success.

Operations

You must keep your business running smoothly. Sometimes too much success can be as troubling as too little. You need to have operations in place to handle these changes and keep everything under control. Operations is often particularly difficult for entrepreneurs. Entrepreneurs tend to be opportunity finders; they often tend to be looking for the next best thing rather than executing details. Operations, on the other hand, is about execution and focusing on details, process, and organization.

A startup company needs to pay particular attention to three crucial business disciplines: finance, product/service development, and sales and marketing. It is important to have one person dedicated to each of these three areas.

As a startup you need to generate revenue quickly. Gearing operations toward this goal is critical. The story of the Erie Canal, arguably the most successful canal ever built, reminds me of this. When construction began in 1817, the "engineers" had a momentous task in front of them: None of them had experience building a canal; the Erie was significantly longer than any previously built in America (363 miles versus only a few miles); and they had to cross swamps and rivers and cut through primeval forests. They ended up constructing the canal through the "Wild West" (remember this is almost 200 years ago) that included the largest stone-arch bridge in the world and a 30-foot-deep channel through solid rock in the days before dynamite, to name a few of their feats – all in eight years. I believe one of their best business decisions was to start on a relatively simple section between Utica and Rome. They learned a lot building this section, and they then started using and collecting tolls on this section while the rest was under construction. This is an important lesson for any enterprise: Start generating revenue as early as possible. This allows you to prove to your stakeholders that you are headed in the right direction, to start collecting information from customers, and to start generating income.

Tying Everything Together

Broken down into its separate parts, as we just discussed, the process of becoming an entrepreneur seems to contain a series of silos, each in isolation from the others. This cannot be the case! The direction, culture, market opportunity, and operations of the company must all be integrated – they must be in alignment, all working as a seamless machine. This alignment must be present so that the culture and operations work smoothly together and both reinforce the marketing message, all working to accomplish the direction. This helps you present a consistent message to all of your stakeholders. You don't want your employees to think you are one type of company, your customers to think of you very differently, and your investors to see you as something else. This is a recipe for disaster.

You must differentiate your offerings for your target market and from your competitors. Looking at your direction, what makes you different from you competitors? Why should a customer buy your product or service? What sets you apart? It is important to think hard about these questions and stress differences that are unique and cannot be easily duplicated by competitors.

Once you have an idea of your differences, it is important to translate your direction, culture, market opportunity, and operations into a coherent message of your key differences to your target audiences. You need to communicate your difference consistently. Every customer contact must communicate your uniqueness. This can be accomplished by aligning your direction, culture, market opportunity, and operations so they work together as parts of a whole, rather than as separate pieces.

Your values should support the key values that customers are looking for. (Be careful here – if you don't believe in a value and cannot make it a core part of who you are, don't pursue it.) Values should interact with operations so your operations can support your unique position in the market and drive you toward your defined direction.

For example, if the main benefit of your product or service is its reliability, then your employees must present themselves in a reliable fashion by doing little things, such as being on time to customer meetings. When the customer sees the entire company as reliable, they will be much more likely to believe the product or service is reliable. At first glance, it might not seem an employee's tardiness for a meeting can disrupt the customer's perception of reliability. But these little actions add up to a perception in the customer's mind.

Think about the last business you used where you experienced truly great service – a business you would recommend without hesitation to a friend. That business has more to offer than the product or service they sell. Did they treat you with respect? Did they reinforce their product or service through actions taken in the entire organization? Think about the little things that made up the entire experience. Most of them probably didn't contribute directly to the end product you received, but did contribute to your overall experience with the business. When you experience a company that is truly aligned, it is very impressive and powerful, especially if this alignment is around uniqueness in the marketplace. These are the types of businesses people talk about and refer friends to.

On the surface, this approach may seem to prevent employees from taking risks or initiative. The opposite is true. When an organization is truly aligned, employees know what is in bounds and what is not. This allows them to take initiative and risks. By setting boundaries for employee actions, you can then let employees act freely, within those boundaries. This promotes accountability, initiative, and empowerment.

It is important, then, to hire people with entrepreneurial spirit. This process should start with the job description and interviews. A great question to ask potential employees, regardless of the job they are applying for, is the "brick question." Simply ask a candidate, "How many bricks are in the average brick house in America?" You will learn a lot about the way a person approaches a problem by how they answer this "simple" question. Once they provide an initial answer, ask, "Can you think of an additional way to answer this question?" This tells you how well someone can think outside the box, how well they can change their mental direction and approach a problem from a new angle. Most people can get one answer; however, the number of people who can come up with a second or third answer is significantly lower.

Once you've found good employees, knowledge-sharing and mentoring foster loyalty, adoption of your culture, and an entrepreneurial spirit. The goal is to make it easy for employees to understand where the company stands, what decisions are being made, and why. For example, your CFO can present the basics of finance to help employees understand the key drivers and how they directly contribute to profitability. It is essential to encourage people to take risks and to reward them even if they fail. Most people are innovative and passionate if they are given opportunity (just look at the hobbies people have), and a lot of businesses miss tapping into their employees' creativity.

Momentum Becomes a Force

When the entire company is working together, you build momentum for success. As all our components work together like a well-oiled machine that is aligned with what customers want, momentum will build. The challenge is to build momentum and not to introduce contradictions that will halt your momentum.

Momentum takes time to build, but once it gets going, it takes on a force of its own. By being consistent in messages differentiated and supported by your operations and culture, you can build momentum for your product or service.

Frederick A. Beer is the cofounder, president, and CEO of Auragen Communications, Inc., based in Rochester, New York. Auragen Communications is a full-service interactive design and development company specializing in Internet, intranet, and extranet solutions for Fortune 1000 companies, whose clients include Eastman Kodak Company, Xerox Corporation, and Frontier Corporation.

Mr. Beer graduated from the University of Rochester with a degree in electrical engineering and a concentration in computer architecture. He started Auragen along with classmate Damir Saracevic directly after graduation. They were soon joined by fellow classmate David Thiel, and Auragen was incorporated on July 25, 1995.

Since its beginnings in a spare bedroom (a little warmer than a garage), Auragen has more than doubled in size every year. Today the company employs 32 developers, designers, copywriters, project managers, and programmers. Auragen was recently recognized as one of the fastest growing private companies in America – debuting at 193 on the Inc. 500 list. Also recognized as one of the Top 100 Web development firms in the country, Auragen has received numerous awards for its work.

Mr. Beer attributes the company's success to its innovative corporate culture and unwavering focus on becoming a national leader in the industry. He believes the culture and structure that the Auragen team has developed is a new model for successful corporations in the information age.

DISCOVERIES: EXPLORING THE WORLD OF ENTREPRENEURIAL MOMENTUM

HATCH GRAHAM
Bandwidth9
Chairman, Chief Executive Officer, and President

How *Not* to Create Entrepreneurial Momentum

Near the end of the 1970s I found myself enjoying a rather comfortable college life, fulfilling my interests with campus attractions, including indulging in the collegiate revelry. Often missing classes, and more than often missing homework assignments, I was the quintessential college "drop-in," motivated merely by a mother's desire to see her son earn a college degree. And, since it was she who had endowed me with a natural gift to run fast and tolerate pain, it seemed only fair that I would entertain the university's offer to barter: one college degree in exchange for several years of scholastic labor. Without clear academic goals, I was promptly fitted for a football uniform.

Engineering was simply a naturally selected path, based on scoring strong marks in the various high school mathematics aptitude tests; candidly, I had discovered multiple choice tests are actually much more probable than random. During my first week of college, the athletic department asked us newly recruited players to declare our curriculum focus. As can be imagined, most of the athletes based their lifelong career ambitions on their past accolades in high school – P.E. class. After hearing four consecutive offensive linemen proudly announce physical education as their major, I went for the gold, and without rhyme or reason, declared nuclear engineering my undergraduate study focus.

Ironically, within one week, and before I could rescind my bluff, I was contacted by the dean of the college of engineering and received a grandfatherly "Welcome aboard! We haven't had a ball player for quite some time!" Reluctantly, I agreed.

For two years, every optional elective was mandated to be replaced by a seemingly endless number of humorless, obscure prerequisite courses focused on such abstract topics as determining the appropriate depth of plunged reactor core rods. This didn't excite me. I reckoned the importance of reactor core rod depth to be essentially the same as roasting a marshmallow – too far away from the campfire and no results; too close to the campfire and she's ablaze.

With no semblance of excitement in the coursework basics, and with my downward trend in attendance rate, it became evident that I was learning the first rule of how *not* to create entrepreneurial momentum. The fundamental flaw was caused by basing a career objective on a superficial desire, which resulted in a level of disinterest that even today is a lasting bad memory.

How to Create Entrepreneurial Momentum

Around the beginning of the 1980s, and about the time of my death spiral of interest, a near tragedy occurred at a nuclear site called Three Mile Island. The country's fondness for anything atomic migrated from intrigue to disdain; it didn't take an economist to see that nuclear-related jobs would be threatened, and upward career mobility would be challenging.

A gifted short-cutter, I began an exhaustive search for something that would provide enjoyment and make a fast-car living. At nearly the same time period, my mother continued her plight of seeing me through the struggle. Innocently, and perfectly, she forwarded a new issue of *National Geographic,* which contained an article about Silicon Valley.

To this day, I can still recall the irony of the article, which on one page featured the world's most complex form of technology at the time (a silicon-based semiconductor wafer), and on the opposing page, featured the quarterly compensatory commission of a high-tech salesman (a brand new, luxurious Mercedes-Benz). Bingo! Count me in.

I feasted on the words of the article, which covered that special blend of sizzling technology combined with the riches to those who delivered it. Apparently, this silicon-related technology could work in time units that were equal to one billionth, and even one trillionth, of a second. The electrical delay required to pass through a logical configuration of transistors required only a few nanoseconds. My farmed-down analogies began working overtime: In one second, light can travel the distance equal to roughly half a dozen trips around the world; in one nanosecond, light travels the width of a pitchfork. The amazing feeling of intrigue, my self-admitted ignorance, and the desire to produce were spectacular. By the end of that week, I had transferred all possible credits away from nuke-ville and prepared to begin a program the engineering college labeled Digital Systems, all part of a standard BSEE degree.

To this day, and after all these years, this series of events remains my most remarkable example of symptomatically identifying the early stages of the creation of entrepreneurial momentum, not something that is mandated, but rather something that evolves from an overwhelming desire to comprehend, produce, and reap reward.

Key Traits of Entrepreneurial Momentum

So far, I had learned the "smart" students were those who continually set the high side of the grading curves, and that they unknowingly grouped themselves into two distinct classifications – those with high levels of experience and those with high levels of intelligence. I despised both, based slightly on self-intimidation and mostly on the way they dressed.

The first smart-student segment was the group who had actually worked in the engineering field prior to, or concurrent with, their formal education. While many of these "work-smart" students were not the brightest bulbs in the lamp, I found them uncomfortably mature, disciplined, and focused on their reason for attending college. They even had the gall to arrive early to class and remain through its entirety.

Work-smart students maintained an unflappable trait of thoroughly completing assignments and double-checking their work. Carelessness was seemingly as evil to them as failing to solve problems quickly. And it was this repetitive and procedural review of their work that I came to respect the most. They were on time, used their knowledge base, and checked their work for accuracy.

The second smart-student segment was just that: extremely smart. These were the socially naive individuals that had perfected the art of being students and were often referred to as "book-smart." They were recognized as being smart as far back as anybody recalled and would continue to be recognized as smart as long as they still had a breath of life, which in some cases was questionable to begin with. Fortunately, the book-smart stereotype often concealed a strong desire to become more normal within social circles – essentially, less smart.

Book-smart students were innocently transparent and certainly easy to communicate with once they saw the relationship as non-threatening to their grade-point average. Although they had an extremely competitive nature, it was typically constrained to within a narrowly defined academic playing field. And, with my inherently non-threatening talent for dumbing-down conversations, I often found myself very compatible with book-smart students.

Book-smart students obligingly showed off their intellectual prowess by stating theoretical reasoning behind complex phenomena, such as Schrödinger's equation, while I would convert it into some ridiculous analogy from my farm life. For example, it was clear that approximating the position of electrons in time should be more complex than approximating the position of a gopher between two mounds; yet, strangely, these remedial representations actually served well to complement the more complex issues. Really.

I became comprehensively aware of the traits of both smart-student groups, partly from a genuine interest in their differentiating characteristics and partly from a need to survive homework assignments. Both types were quick to provide tutorial assistance, as it created yet another intellectual stage on which to perform. At the time, I found it appealing that I could meander my way through virtually any coursework, using my bond-to-smart-student technique, and conveniently wait just long enough so that my smart associates confidently understood the subject matter. Then, by quickly "getting up to speed" through a focused debriefing or two, I would be prepared just in time before randomly scheduled tests might reveal my lack of effort.

At a point about midway through my undergraduate program, I finally had to "meet my maker" in a sense. Through an unlikely dialogue with a professor notorious for flunking students (and usually following up with a callous disinterest in their pleadings for grade relief), I found myself at his door whimpering for reconsideration. After he failed to take the bait during the customary 50-yard-line-tickets bribe, I was certain to be merely the turkey entertaining the pilgrim on Thanksgiving Day.

However, in a most uncharacteristic chain of events, I became stymied by something even worse than the professor's typical lack of concern. First, without hesitation, he adjusted my grade up to a passing level and, second, delivered a *force majeure* blow in the form of a condescending but overdue proclamation:

"Graham, someday you will learn you cannot get by on boyish good looks and charm. This world requires work."

At that moment, I began my search to create "my" form of student, one who might combine my style – typically searching for the fastest and easiest path – with occasionally solid work ethics. I might be able to search for the fastest and easiest path – to meet an objective! The jig was up; my cover was blown. A strong work ethic would be needed.

It Takes All Kinds

Confident that I would never be able to emulate either of the two "smart" student groups, I thought perhaps I could integrate myself with them, in the form of an ally. At first, it seemed a highly contradictory notion. But after refining that process, I was becoming more and more focused on developing processes that would enable me to trust my smart allies, learn quickly, be creative, and perform well. Having become more confident in this unconventional relationship, I thought I might even be able to use my impatient style (that always searched for the creative shortcut) to actually enhance the performance of my smart counterparts. Then, by adding an occasional solid work ethic into the equation, I would ensure a level of mutual respect and credibility, resulting in a lasting bond.

Admittedly, this would mean I would never be able to perform alone and would always need to address goals from a team or alliance orientation – a tough requirement, considering that I would need to give up my symbolic he-man gestures of shoving the smart students aside in the hallways. The presumed thought of needing to behave was overwhelming; fortunately, it never became a constant requirement.

Moving forward, my reputed talent for barely squeaking by was beginning to become blemished by the success of this interesting enterprise. I was gaining a better comprehension of the subject matter, and to their surprise, the smart students were actually learning how to visibly identify the difference between an offensive pro-set and a tier formation at the football games.

The use of this peculiar and suspicious relationship model became my own form of getting along, my own form of team dependency. To this day it is the driving energy behind virtually every aspect of my professional career – in essence, the means to rely heavily on three types of human talent: those who are experienced, those who are brilliant, and those who creatively search for the most efficient path to success. It has been a primary key to creating and sustaining entrepreneurial momentum.

"Ideal Opportunity" for Entrepreneurial Momentum?

At the beginning of the 1990s I was thriving in a company that conducted business primarily with the U.S. Department of Defense. The company also had other business concerns with various agencies of the government, but the nature of that work was not readily disclosed. Having successfully manipulated my way into the intellectual community, I caught on quickly that U.S. government intelligence, in the form of technology, is considered "special," especially since most of the work deliverables were sent to postal boxes somewhere in Maryland or Virginia, and to recipients randomly named Bob or Jim. And, depending on the day of the week, the names would change, as well as the addresses. I didn't ask; they didn't tell.

The positive side of such dark, spoof-oriented activities was in the technology. I'd become well-versed in the art of integrated circuit design and manufacturing, and my perspective as a project manager was initially motivated by the appealing performance of the leading-edge communications technology in which the company was involved. In addition, to my good fortune, the smart-student concept of my college days parlayed perfectly into an updated "smart-engineer" scheme during my professional days – experienced engineers and brilliant engineers.

In a fascinating way, some of the projects seemed to have been driven by old episodes of "Star Trek" or bygone days of "Dick Tracy," but through the unity of my smart-engineering team, coupled with my creative impatience, we displayed a level of committed confidence that helped us achieve virtually everything we attempted (or accosted). One project joined an array of world-class communications scientists and me to develop a terrestrial radio that could transmit and receive signals around the world using outer-space meteor bursts as reflectors of the signals. Granted, the volume of "users" of such a powerful and expensive product would be limited, but at intellectual cocktail parties, when the question came up of what I did for a living, meteor-burst communications was certain to secure my position at the top of the totem pole – even rocket scientists would have to applaud.

I'm confident of this because of my earlier involvement with another project: developing a guidance system within a ballistic missile – the science of guiding a rocket! Although qualifying me for rocket scientist status, my farmed-down comparison of the effort was not popular among the sponsoring military brass. Apparently, comparing their prestigious guidance system to "sighting in my old Remington for the big turkey shoot" did not adequately support the perceived complexity that requires a billion-dollar budget. And, after I learned how to override the Anti-Spoof-Selective-Availability of the Global Positioning System (which enabled directing a missile to within a few centimeters), my boasting of being able to "split a hair on a rat's bottom" secured my removal from future presentations.

However, aside from my poor-country-boy representations of such sophisticated programs, the clarity of success was astounding. Our unique blend of experienced engineers, brilliant scientists, and creative impatience was impressing not only clients, but also industry analysts and major shareholders. And, having submersed myself under some of the world's most advanced technology efforts, I resurfaced with a firm belief that there is no ideal opportunity for entrepreneurial momentum. Instead, entrepreneurial momentum can actually thrive in any environment where there's a valid need for a solution to a problem – even environments funded by customers known only as Bob or Jim with post boxes in Virginia or Maryland.

Inspiration for Entrepreneurial Momentum

With no place for the corporate powers-that-be to hide me, I was shortly thereafter "awarded" general management status of the company's integrated circuit division, which did not yet exist. With the promotion came the introduction to the fundamentally basic element of business: *profit.* Most important from a personal standpoint, profit performance leads to higher corporate executive bonuses.

Although I had not yet understood the necessary financial principles behind a company's valuation and its earnings, I still maintained that this knowledge of profit versus personal wealth dependency was my in-absentia Harvard MBA. Nothing ever spoke such volumes of business strategy as the relationship between an executive bonus and a dollar of profit – certainly not my Harvard MBA acquaintances I'll loosely refer to as friends.

Quickly, a change of strategy was needed in the selection of projects to pursue, projects that could yield enough profit to reward the smart engineers and me with substantial bonuses. Otherwise, my new promotion would simply be positioning me as a "big hat with no cattle."

Adverse Effects on Entrepreneurial Momentum

After strenuous thrashings of my smart engineers, demanding that they derive commercially viable, highly profitable products, I quickly found that very rarely does entrepreneurial momentum begin with the solution – it was clear we first needed to find a problem. Furthermore, because my then-current disposition of impatience lacked the necessary creative counterpart, my smart engineers were beginning to growl, as in an underground language they had secretly saved for a patriotic revolt against establishment. Deciphering this curious form of expression among engineers is like tracking a mule deer in snow: Once the snow melts, there's no sign left to track – but that doesn't mean the buck has left the area.

Smart engineers have the same elusive skill of avoiding outward discontent, and once detected, it often disappears quickly. Unfortunately, it takes a much longer time to truly diminish, and without properly decoding the early symptoms, the entrepreneurial momentum can be dramatically and adversely affected. Considering the importance of fostering the bonds among the three groups of talent (brilliant engineer, experienced engineer, creative impatient), if the morale of one group weakens, the team becomes unstable.

Another mistake encountered during this period was a misguided deviation from my self-proclaimed "perfect model" for creating and sustaining entrepreneurial momentum. Candidly, I doubted the necessity of incorporating all three traits in all circumstances. In essence, my own preference would at times "lean" the mix of staff on certain projects more heavily toward my style and behavior, and I would omit one or the other smart groups from the team. Those projects succeeded in establishing a perfect record of failure, based on schedule, performance, or cost difficulties. A basic presumption suggests that the lack of the appropriate team ingredients substantially causes an instability or lack of balance within the team – something like a fat man on a two-legged stool.

The Final Ingredient in Entrepreneurial Momentum

Over time, as the "perfect model" evolved, the recipe for success also adapted. Fundamentally, the combination of smart-engineer and creative-impatient types conclusively formed my opinion on the essential formula for maximizing entrepreneurial momentum. In addition, not all things in life are certain – which, of course, is an understatement. In fact, I have found that no entrepreneurial activity is without uncertainty; the world's most prolific companies have been laced with change and uncertainty, without exception.

In 1991, after we'd built a series of small but highly visible telecommunications business units, an opportunity presented a remarkable example of the promise, risk, and enormous reward of uncertainty. A routine sales call regarding our line of satellite communication products came with a request for information from a substantial company. The request was highly unrelated to satellite communications, but because of the size of the customer, we gave a generous level of credence to the interest.

The challenge was to develop a way to send signals over coaxial cable. Initially, because of the extreme level of uncertainty, the obvious reaction was to dismiss the opportunity based on its apparent lack of applicability to the existing products. What could possibly be similar between signals sent between the earth and spacecraft, and signals sent over coaxial cable? To help appease our uncertainty, the client offered to provide the necessary cable TV application experience we lacked, which indicated this opportunity was quite substantial. However, although the gift horse was offered, we'd still need to have a look at the teeth.

An obligatory review meeting yielded astonishing information. First, the application was within a market that served 60 million households in the U.S. – the cable TV market – and the effort was to ascertain the ease of migrating a satellite communications transmitter design into a cable TV set-top box. The application would be to enable homes to actually do more than simply receive television programming, but would also transmit information back "up" to the network. If this could be accomplished, cable carriers could also provide telephony and data services, and begin competing for virtually every type of interactive application to homes, as opposed to being constrained to video-related services. As might be imagined, this effort had more than its share of uncertainty, but also exhibited an enormous value if the problem could be solved.

By means of an introductory assessment of how our capabilities and technology could serve this need, we reduced the uncertainty to a manageable level. We subsequently assembled a team that consisted of brilliance, creative impatience, and, through partnership with the client, experience. The result was the world's first, and still predominant, technology for transmitting information "upstream" from homes within the cable modem market. The return on the investment decision, through intellectual property fees and revenue-generated profit, was in excess of 3,000 percent within five years. Through properly managing uncertainty, the entrepreneurial momentum that was created enabled the project to become one of the most successful, rewarding efforts in the company's 20-year history.

As in this example, uncertainty often forces substantial change, and the ability to accept and embrace change is an issue of resources, both human and monetary. Quite often the uncertainty of standards, consumer demand, supply sources, and an endless supply of dynamic conditions will factor into entrepreneurial momentum. And, understanding that every valuable solution first needs a costly problem, the ability to "screen for profit" becomes an important exercise in gauging uncertainty. Without a doubt, one of the most important elements to manage throughout the entire cycle of creating and maintaining entrepreneurial momentum is uncertainty. It encompasses all of the aspects of an opportunity that can create fame and fortune, or failure and disgrace, including risks of time, cost, technology, and talent.

Hatch Graham joined Bundwidth9 in June 2000 as chairman, CEO, and president. He spent the previous year guiding startups and early-stage companies, during which time each of his five primary companies achieved an average valuation growth of over 500 percent.

Before Mr. Graham's venture activities, he held the position of group president of World Access, an Atlanta-based telecommunications company. From the time he joined the company in early 1997 to mid-1999, when he resigned to pursue startup ventures, the company realized revenue growth of over 500 percent, with an annualized run rate of more than $600 million.

Preceding World Access, Mr. Graham served as senior vice president of TCSI Corporation, where he led the efforts to stabilize and refocus the company's ailing imbedded software business. After the company's successful transition back to profitability, he successfully sold the business unit. He was also a key to TCSI's increase in market capitalization from $150 million to more than $700 million within six months of his joining the company. Before TCSI Mr. Graham held the position of corporate vice president of Stanford Telecom. Within two years from inception, his business units in wireless, cable TV, and satellite products were responsible for raising the market capitalization of Stanford Telecom over 400 percent, and they were profitable every year.

Mr. Graham has represented his companies in key financial events, such as early- and late-stage private equity rounds, convertible debt financings, public offerings, and a variety of road shows. As a technologist, he has patents for architectures for direct digital synthesis, programmable logic device, digital filtering, forward error correction, spread spectrum, cable TV, and cellular telephone applications. At Stanford Telecom, he received a coveted "reverse path" patent for CATV bi-directional communications, as well as an error correction patent that contributed to the introduction of direct broadcast satellite television.

Mr. Graham has been session chairman and key speaker at several industry symposiums and trade shows. EE Times, *a leading industry journal, published a feature article about him in their 20th anniversary issue, calling Mr. Graham "a true force behind our industry." He graduated in 1982 with a BSEE degree from Idaho State University, where he serves on the I.S.U. College of Engineering advisory council and which awarded him the university's prestigious Professional Achievement Award.*

THE EXTREME
ENTREPRENEUR

TODD PARENT
Extreme Pizza
Chief Executive Officer

The Extreme Concept

Of a character or kind farthest removed from the ordinary or average: *extreme pizza entrepreneur.*

To have an extremely successful restaurant, you need extremely good employees, products, and ideas and an *extreme* vision. This is exactly what I had in mind when I opened the first Extreme Pizza location in San Francisco, California, in 1994. My concept was to incorporate an extreme sports theme with pizza and cultivate an extremely motivated and enthusiastic staff. The results have been a concept that is expanding into numerous states.

I am driven to the utmost extremes to provide a great product and unsurpassed service. I strive to be a leader in a fast-paced and growing business, highly respected by the entire staff, and a true role model for all who meet me. I have merged my athletics and hard work and have made a career combining these two greatest passions: sports and food.

My first inclination as a child was to push my limits as an athlete, and I quickly excelled at many sports – skiing, biking, sailing, surfing, windsurfing, kite sailing, tennis, paddle – all with the fierce edge of competition. Over the years I took every opportunity to learn more sports and perfect my skills. My enthusiasm for being the best in whatever sport I choose crosses over to my quest for excellence in Extreme Pizza.

Extreme Pizza evolved from my love of "extreme" sports, and the theme of the store is exactly that. The walls of the restaurants are covered with photos of extreme surfers, bikers, windsurfers, canoers, skiers – many of whom are friends of mine – performing outrageous feats. So while customers are enjoying some of the cleverly named gourmet pizza combinations – an Everest, a Fear Factor, an Endless Summer, or a Fresh Tracks – they can also enjoy sports on the TV and the amazing stacks of food that Extreme Pizza offers. Customers can happily feel they are pushing the limits of extremely delicious eating!

Extreme Listening

I am a working example of the grassroots leadership and hands-on dedication that have permitted Extreme Pizza to overcome growing pains and emerge as a flourishing business. By maintaining flexibility in the business model and always listening to the root of Extreme's success – its customers – the company has reworked concepts and given new meaning to being a survivor in the evolving marketplace.

I started Extreme Pizza as a take-and-bake operation where customers would take home unbaked pizzas to cook in their own ovens. Customers requested cooked pizzas delivered fresh and hot to their doors and charged to their credit cards. I acquiesced to the customers' desires and changed the store policies. Baked pizzas now account for over 73 percent of revenue. Delivery and credit card charges were not available at the outset. Now, more than 70 percent of sales stem from delivery, and approximately

40 percent of business come from credit card charges. I have learned to adapt the business model of my company to fit the needs of the marketplace Extreme Pizza serves.

This ability to listen and respond to customers' requests has led to Extreme Pizza's financial and operational success.

The Birth of a Business

The concept for Extreme Pizza originated in France in 1987, when I was studying at the Sorbonne during my junior year in college. The flocks of Parisians gathering at crepe stands for a delicious meal-to-go intrigued me. I foresaw the demand in the U.S. for a healthier and more gourmet alternative to typical American fast food.

After getting my degree in economics at the University of Vermont and working on Wall Street in New York, I decided it was time to fulfill my dream. I started by learning every aspect of the restaurant business and working all the shifts and stations at various restaurants. I grasped the intricacies of every position from dishwashing, cooking, bartending, and serving, to managing, and I quickly learned that no job was easy. My training for my career in the food business resembled my attitude toward life: Do everything to its fullest potential; realize mistakes; and move forward with this learned experience.

Unlike many recent startup companies that began with a huge expense account and managed to fizzle everything away,

Extreme Pizza has endured and thrived. I have remained frugal as I have grown the business. At the same time, I have never lost sight of the most important aspect of the food industry: consistency in product and service. Under this philosophy, when you are extreme, nothing less is expected.

Turning Employees into Entrepreneurs

If you ask me which aspect of the business is most important, I would answer without qualification, "The Extreme Team." I am fiercely proud of the entire staff and their enthusiasm for what they do – a relative rarity in the restaurant business. I listen to all of the employees, knowing that many of the business's most creative and useful ideas come from the people who operate in-store, since they are the ones who interact most closely with the customers.

My goal is to empower every employee of Extreme Pizza with decision-making responsibility. This philosophy has reflected a positive and upbeat spin of the company's growth. Employees remain excited and motivated; they continue push their limits of learning and, in turn, become entrepreneurs in their own right.

I realize the importance of cultivating new experts in the stores and am eager to train employees and advance people to help prepare them for leadership roles in the company. I have learned the significance of allowing the team to make decisions and to learn from their own mistakes. In this way, they create learning experiences to improve performance throughout the entire company. This methodology entices people to join, to stay – and to perform.

Extreme Pizza invests time and money in its employees. I have put in place several incentive plans designed to encourage employees to work hard and remain loyal to the company. Many of the values that are respected by upper management are often an interpretation of dedication. Some of these are initiative, aggressiveness, loyalty, adherence to company policy, desire for excellence, personal growth, and a positive attitude toward the company.

I have also instituted an active training program for all store managers. This ongoing mentoring system ensures a sincere interest in the employees and recognizes their potential for growth. Educating the managers on the corporate goals and visions has resulted in a staff that is working toward those goals. As a company, Extreme Pizza has strived to cut the cost of goods, scaled down on labor percentages, and increase revenue. To help instill these goals, during the Extreme Pizza weekly managers' meetings, a weekly competition is held among all of its retail stores. A cash bonus is paid to the store that has best reached the established criteria. This not only creates some excitement, but also keeps the managers working toward the company goals.

There are many different jobs in the market, and Extreme Pizza strives to remain competitive. I constantly research what other job opportunities are available and what they offer their employees. I stay on the cutting edge of what Extreme Pizza can provide for each employee. This builds loyalty with the employees and allows Extreme Pizza to maintain a well-trained, efficient, and hard-working staff.

I recognize that my job as a leader is to provide an environment in which people are not only *able* to do well, but *want* to do well – so well, it's extreme!

Innovative Approaches to Extreme Beginnings

I encourage innovation and the flow of creative ideas into my business. This is a continuous cycle that never stops and contributes to the ongoing success of the company. New approaches to doing business better are always being discussed, and Extreme Pizza moves to implement these ideas when it makes the most sense.

In the early days of Extreme Pizza, when the marketing budget was small, I promoted the store myself when I was not busy making pizza. This ingenuity landed me many grassroots marketing campaigns that incorporated techniques that are still productive for the company today. I pioneered the concept of "Extreme" cross-promotion programs with local retailers, such as enter-to-win contests and Web-based sales incentive programs with discounts and coupons. Extreme Pizza has hosted several events and given many presentations to introduce our pizzas to new customers.

I have also put Extreme Pizza at the forefront of active community involvement, working closely with local schools and charitable organizations. The company participates in parades, community fairs, and city donations and strives to improve neighborhood aesthetics. Once a month, Extreme Pizza invites a grade school to a store where the staff demonstrates how to make a pizza and allows the children to make a pizza and enjoy it for lunch. Teachers, kids, and parents appreciate the efforts the store makes to become involved in the community and in turn support the business.

When Extreme Pizza opened its doors on Shattuck Avenue in Berkeley, California, it had the distinction of being the first restaurant to be certified by the Green Business Program in Alameda County. When I began laying the plans for the new Berkeley restaurant, I envisioned creating a "green" eatery. I covered all the bases for reducing energy, water, and materials consumption, including using safer cleaners and installing furniture made from used skis and snow boards. All of the store's paper products, including the pizza delivery boxes, are made of recycled fiber. The staff works to minimize all food waste and donates leftover food to local charities.

I also recognize the importance of the corporate market to my business's success. Corporations are some of Extreme Pizza's best customers, and I have put processes in place that entice corporate customers to keep coming back for more. Not only do business customers appreciate Extreme's excellent customer service, fast delivery, and fresh gourmet product, but they also appreciate an expedited ordering process that makes it easy to order Extreme Pizza for large corporate events. Extreme Pizza created the option for companies to open accounts with the stores. Instead of discussing payment options when the order is placed, Extreme Pizza invoices the company for orders and allows for payment at a later date. Many companies appreciate this service and call or fax in orders, since this option is available, too. These innovative practices in the community and in the corporate market have produced phenomenal results for Extreme Pizza.

Hiring the Extreme Employee

The greatest team on earth has come handpicked. When hiring new employees, whether for management or operations, I look for people who emanate confidence and the ability to take responsibility. I want someone who will speak freely in an interview and who is able to hold an intelligible conversation. Finding the newest member of the Extreme Team requires some skill, since I seek long-term employees. Each employee completes an intensive training period in which both the management team and the new hire learn quickly whether this is a good fit.

Since all the employees work closely with the customers, I place importance on honesty, professionalism, sincerity, and hospitality. The Extreme Team looks for smart, hard-working employees with similar work ethics and motivation for success. These ideals are an intricate part of the continued growth of the company.

I focus great emphasis on hiring the best managers – those who have an entrepreneurial spirit and are willing to work hard for the success of the company. The store managers know specifically what duties need to be done to run a smooth shift, and they hire people they can trust to work in their stores. This hiring system promotes mutual respect and an entire team working toward the same goals.

I acknowledge the hard work and dedication of the *entire* Extreme Team – general managers, store managers, preparation crew, cashiers, drivers, and of course, the glorious Extreme pizza makers!

Extreme Advice

In my earlier years in the restaurant business, one of my mentors shared with me a motto that I have since adopted as my own: Perseverance, persistence, dedication, and the love for what you do will allow you success. I love what I do every day. I am dedicated to the Extreme Team and the success of the entire company.

I advise other entrepreneurs to set goals that exceed your expectations. If you achieve them, you have grown your company. Aiming higher produces greater results and allows for more growth and creativity.

As a leader, I stress the need to be a good listener and to respond to what you hear. The Golden Rule is having passion for whatever you are doing. I continue every day, excited to pursue this goal. I also surround myself with people who share a similar interest and passion.

Over the years I have refined my ability to delegate effectively so employees are able to expand their knowledge base. Furthermore, it is imperative to let employees manage their own projects and allow them to flourish with your company, as well. As the leader, I try to be a source of support and inspiration to the entire Extreme Team.

Keeping an Extreme Edge

For any business to maintain a competitive edge, it must always be aware of what the competition is doing. I still visit local pizza restaurants to see how they are running their businesses and what their strengths and weaknesses are, and to learn how Extreme Pizza can offer better products and services.

Most important, I listen – listen to the staff and to the customers. In my view, the employees provide the most valuable feedback for Extreme Pizza. Since the employees are in constant interaction with customers, staff members are in a good position to provide valuable advice and feedback on how to improve the business. If staff members bring up new ideas, questions, or concerns, it is most likely because the Extreme Pizza customers are demanding more. I still read the customer comment cards that are filled out in the store to get a read on what customers think.

Extreme Future

I will summarize Extreme Pizza's business plan in a word: growth. Some of the goals for Extreme Pizza include expanding in-store sales, increasing customer base, augmenting marketing capacity, broadening our name recognition, increasing repeat customers, and developing new business in new markets.

I have tried to assuage growing pains by implementing systems to manage business processes in a timely and efficient manner. Creating management procedures and regulation modules helps to ease hiring, training, and promotion transitions. I have also been a strong advocate of new technology, which we use to take orders, process spreadsheets, report sales numbers, and analyze growth charts.

A reciprocal interest for growth exists with the investors pursuing franchising opportunities with Extreme Pizza. This desire for expansion is a reality with franchise interest around the country.

I have indeed carved out a niche in the pizza industry. With an enticing business concept, highly motivated employees, and a desire to reach the "extreme" in products and service, Extreme Pizza is on the road to great success. This is a company to keep an eye on, to join, or at the very least, to visit for an unforgettable slice.

Todd Parent was born in 1966 in Long Branch, New Jersey. Growing up in a small coastal town, Mr. Parent began swimming, surfing, and sailboarding at a young age. His competitive nature drove him toward many other sports, including tennis, skateboarding, biking, soccer, and skiing – many of which he still plays today. This motivational spirit also helped him excel in his academic studies.

Mr. Parent graduated with a Bachelor of Arts degree in economics and with a French literature minor from The University of Vermont in 1988. After a brief stint with the banking world at U.S. Trust in New York City, he quickly realized he needed a more active and healthful lifestyle incorporated in his workplace. He then began training in the restaurant business to pursue his dream to become a successful entrepreneur.

After learning many of the intricacies of the restaurant industry, he found his niche with Extreme Pizza. The company has a reputation for its innovative pizza combinations, using only the finest ingredients, and its philosophy: Extreme, not mainstream. Extreme Pizza stands behind its motto, "Life Is Too Short For Mediocrity," and ensures extreme delivery, extreme customer service, and extreme dining.

Mr. Parent has guided Extreme Pizza to set the standard within the pizza industry for top-quality service, freshness, texture, flavor, and variety. The results are paying off – in 2001 Extreme Pizza was ranked #22 of 150 fastest-growing private companies by the San Francisco Business Times, and in 2002 Extreme Pizza was ranked #42. Inc. 500 named Extreme Pizza #241 of the Fastest Privately Held Companies in 2001. Mr. Parent was a finalist for Ernst & Young's Entrepreneur of the Year Award in 2001, and he was featured in the East Bay Business Times' "40 under 40" in 2002. San Francisco Weekly voted Extreme Pizza the "Best Pizza in San Francisco" in 1998. And to show a little Extreme Pizza love far away from home, the Calgary Sun in Alberta, Canada, gave Extreme Pizza high accolades for being the most delicious pizza ever.

A BLUEPRINT FOR LONG-TERM SUCCESS

FARSHEED FERDOWSI
PayMaxx
President and Chief Executive Officer

Gaining Traction as a New Business

Having many years of experience in the business-to-business (B2B) arena, I believe the approach to gaining traction is different in B2B versus retail and other industries. In fact, if you pose the question, "What does it take for a new business to gain traction?" to a group of business students in any prestigious business school and restrict them to answer you in one or two words, you will see my point. The students will invariably respond with "capital," "business plan," "employees," "product," "marketing," etc. Conversely, if you ask the same question of a group of B2B entrepreneurs, you will quickly get the most accurate answer – "a customer!" In the business services industry, your first customer is the single most important requirement for a business to take hold. Everything else – important as it may be – is secondary.

To gain traction as a new business you must, by any legitimate means possible, get that first customer. You might have to discount your product and services heavily. You might have to sell your first customer at a loss. You might even have to customize your product for your first customer's specific needs. You must however, get him signed up.

Once this is done, you must shower that customer with service: Free on-site product training? *Of course!*
Direct phone line to you, the owner? *No problem!*
Sixty-day terms? *Absolutely!*

You have only a precious few months to WOW the first (reference) customer. All along, you should make sure your reference customer clearly understands there are two conditions for being treated so well.

The customer must understand and acknowledge that his terms of service are confidential. This keeps future customers from demanding the same terms and also makes the reference customer feel extra special.

Also, it is in your mutual best interest for this reference customer to assist you in obtaining additional customers.

Leveraging this reference customer, you press on to get your next four customers. While still piling on special services, you must be sure you service these four new customers at break-even or at a slight profit. Having five paying customers on a basic break-even level would be the foundation for a successful enterprise.

When you have five customers, you then begin advertising with a modest campaign. Word-of-mouth is the best method of hooking additional customers. One effective technique is to persuade your five paying customers to each commit to bringing one new customer onboard. They will be glad to help you. You can reward them by special discounts toward future purchases. Call them and thank them if they bring you new customers. Share your successes with your first cluster of customers. Every entrepreneur loves to see another one succeed.

After the first 10 or so customers are onboard, you can be sure you have a proven concept. Now, to grow it, you must begin a determined analysis of your business and your market to devise a strategy for growth and profitability. Devising a strategy to grow your business requires the following fundamental understandings:

1. You must understand the revenue drivers of your business.

Each business has its own revenue drivers. Revenue drivers are the aspects of your business that provide the basis for your revenues. They are the alphabets of growth of your business. If you manage these revenue drivers correctly, the revenue itself will naturally follow.

In the payroll business, where I have spent my energies for the past 10 years, the revenue drivers are the client employee census (the number of our customers' active employees) and revenue yield per payroll check. In the restaurant business the revenue drivers may be customer count and average check. In a computer-learning center the revenue drivers may be the number of students enrolled and average training fee per student. This type of analysis will help you determine the two or three most important parameters that contribute to the growth of your business. You will then have a target at which to aim. You should single out these parameters and attack them – relentlessly. Pursue them passionately. Monitor and chart their growth. Celebrate milestones reached. Share the good news with your staff, friends, family, and customers.

When you find yourself waking up in the middle of the night (either elated or in a cold sweat) thinking about your revenue drivers, you have achieved passion for your business. You are on your way to success.

2. You must understand the concept of product lifecycles.

Every living thing in the universe follows a similar lifecycle. At birth it is small, weak, and vulnerable, but it grows rapidly. During youth it has substance, and it continues to grow, but it lacks structure and discipline. At maturity its growth slows; yet a marked improvement in quality, stability, and structure is observed. This is followed by age, marked by rigidity, decline, and obsolescence. The final stage is death, characterized by perfect stillness and decay.

Human life, civilizations, corporations, and products – all alike – follow this pattern. The astute entrepreneur fully understands this and devises methodologies to counter its effects. As applied to products, the only way to counter this is continuous innovation and reinvention. As soon as product A has reached youth, you must introduce product B as an infant. By the time Product A has reached maturity and Product B is in its youth, you must release Product C as a new infant product. Successive product releases, timed correctly, will save your business from decline, age, obsolesce, and death. You can grow perpetually as long as the pipeline of innovation is full. It is also important to understand that the lifecycle is different from industry to industry and even from product to product.

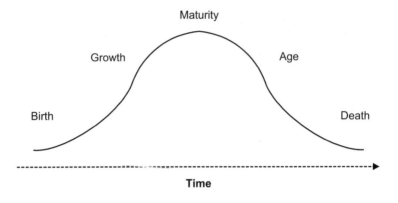

3. You must determine your competitive advantage.

Competition and competitive advantage are always based on quality, service, and price. They can be described as follows:

❑ *Quality:* features, functionality, accuracy, technology
❑ *Service:* timeliness, flexibility, concern, human contact
❑ *Price:* dollar amount, terms, structure, simplicity, stability

As an entrepreneur, you must pick two out of these three competitive advantages. One factor alone will not do, and competing on all three is impossible. Any combination of two will suffice, depending on how you wish to compete in your industry. You can compete based on:

High Quality/High Service (Tavern on the Green, NY)
This strategy requires you to charge higher prices to provide good quality and service. When dining at Tavern on the Green, you will be certain to receive an excellent meal with excellent service, but you will most certainly spend more for it.

110

High Quality/Good Price (Café du Monde, New Orleans)
This strategy requires you to sacrifice a certain amount of service to meet the other two aspects of your model. For example, the Café du Monde is renowned for offering high-quality coffees and beignets in the French Quarter at very reasonable prices, but the lines are enormous.

High Service/Good Price (McDonald's)
This strategy caters to a specific, serviceable aspect of the customer, while maintaining a low price. McDonald's doesn't have filet mignon anywhere on the menu, but the pre-prepared hamburgers are inexpensive and convenient when you're in a hurry.

These companies are successful in the way they choose to compete. All of these models are fiercely competitive but are based on different permutations of those three basic competitive factors. After you determine your combination, you must actually behave accordingly and build an organization that reflects and projects that advantage. It would be disastrous to have service as one of your competitive advantages and not invest heavily in a customer service team. Similarly, your claims of quality would sound hollow if you use the cheapest raw materials, pay little or no attention to the packaging, and ignore quality control.

The theory behind these competitive factors is that there is a specific interplay between them that customers intuitively use to determine which product or service offers the best value. The interplay is best described in the following equation:

Customer Value = (Quality X Service) / Price

Suppose a customer is considering three alternative vendors for a long-term building maintenance contract. The customer has done his homework and has requested written proposals from three reputable firms. Which firm will win this contract? Is it the lowest bidder? Is it the best service provider? The answer is most likely the highest *value* provider. Let's go through this as a hypothetical exercise.

The astute, value-conscious customer averages the annual price of the three bids and then divides each price into that average to obtain "relative price" ratios. The customer continues by assigning a relative score to the *quality* of the service (measured by the certifications of the technicians, dispatch technology deployed, quality of parts used, etc.). Similarly, the customer assigns relative scores for the *service* level of each vendor (measured by guaranteed response time, customer satisfaction surveys, etc.). The result of this analysis will look somewhat like the following table:

Vendor	Relative Price	Relative Quality	Relative Service	Customer Value	
A	1.18	1.5	2.0	2.5	**Winner!**
B	0.96	1.3	1.5	2.0	
C	0.86	1.0	0.9	1.0	

Note the highest-price bidder wins the *value* proposition and the bid. Why? Because he is competing based on quality and service, so he charges a higher price to provide it. The lowest bidder came in last. Why? Because his price is so low he cannot provide good service and high quality.

4. *You must articulate your differentiation.*

Without differentiation, prospects for growth are very limited. You can differentiate your product/service offering based on a number of factors. Chief among these are:

Specific technology/feature sets can be valuable. What does your product do better than anyone else's product? If you cannot think of anything, you will have a problem growing your business. If you can think of several, then you should identify the most important one or two and drive them home in all of your presentations and marketing efforts. Examples of this kind of marketing include the reliability symbolized by the bored Maytag repairman, or Domino's Pizza's guaranteed delivery of a hot pizza in less than 30 minutes. These things were conceived to separate the companies from their competition.

A unique business model can be a powerful differentiator. Domino's Pizza has only delivery. That they do not have dine-in (like Pizza Hut) can be articulated as a unique business model that is more focused and efficient.

At PayMaxx, we do not accept responsibility for payroll data entry. Customers have to perform their own data entry via the Internet or a PC-input device. This has provided us great efficiencies, which makes us more competitive. The client who traditionally had to transcribe his payroll hours onto a form to call it in or fax it in spends the same amount of time entering it into a browser (or PC) and transmitting it to us. Data integrity and accuracy are significantly higher, and clients are empowered to ensure the accuracy of their own data. Everyone wins, and a powerful differentiation is created and articulated.

Special bundling/pricing is the oldest trick in the differentiation game. "Buy this equipment, and we will throw in the installation." "Buy this car, and we will offer you zero financing." "Rent this apartment for two years, and we will give you the first three months free." Examples are endless.

At PayMaxx, we have experimented with a whole series of special pricing and bundling schemes. In the beginning, our fixed-monthly-fee promotion was very successful. All of our competitors priced their services on a per-transaction basis. That meant the client was charged for every single transaction. Every check, direct deposit, garnishment, tax deposit, you name it, was considered a transaction. Any client with more than a few dozen employees was being overwhelmed by transaction fees. By offering a fixed, once-a-month charge to our clients, we differentiated ourselves, and our customers loved us. This unique and revolutionary pricing scheme carried PayMaxx in its early years and gave us a solid footing in the industry.

Today, we aren't forced to offer that kind of blanket pricing, but we do offer a variation. In addition to the traditional transactional pricing, we provide the client the option of a flat fee per active employee. Under this regimen we charge the client a variable, once-a-month fee based on the number of active employees they have. If their rate is $4 per employee per month, then we simply count the number of employees and send the client a bill. This helps us because as our customers grow, so does our revenue. A client's bill increases (or decreases) based on their need, rather than some rigid contract. Having this kind of differentiation means our sales consultants have a powerful story to tell. It also leaves our larger competitors shell-shocked.

To entice the smaller clients (fewer than 100 employees), we offer free year-end W-2s. This is another pricing strategy perceived as a huge incentive for customers that costs us only $50 per customer, per year. We know this to be a solid strategy by the number of clients who cite this as one of the reasons they left our competition and switched to PayMaxx.

Industry specialization and experience make customers feel comfortable. They are often impressed if you understand their industry and are familiar with their unique lingo. If you can gain such knowledge or familiarity, you can leverage it as a powerful differentiator. At PayMaxx, we used our expertise in franchised restaurant operations to position ourselves as experts in providing payroll services to clients with multiple worksites.

Accomplishments, awards, and recognition can make your name recognizable. In all cities and major metropolitan areas there are various awards and recognitions available from the Chamber of Commerce, the Small Business Administration, local banks, etc. Find out about these and apply for them. If you qualify and win any of these recognitions, prepare a press release and send it to all the local newspapers, as well as your customers. This action

115

has a tendency to snowball. Soon you will be called for quotes; you may be invited to speak at trade shows or invited to serve on panel discussions. All such awards and recognitions should be leveraged to gain customer trust and respect, which ultimately fuels growth.

PayMaxx has been inducted into Nashville's Future 50 Hall of Fame after winning that award five years in a row. We have made the Inc. 500 list four consecutive years. We have won *Smart Business* magazine's MVP (Most Valuable Product) award for 2001 for our Internet Payroll service, PowerPayroll.com. We make sure all of our marketing collateral, Web sites, and customer presentations mention these achievements. A powerful differentiator indeed!

5. You must devise a marketing strategy for growth.

Strategy is a military term, which in its simplest form means, "organizing one's assets to one's maximum advantage." This said, and after clearly understanding the above fundamentals, a growth strategy can be devised by providing answers to the following questions:

❏ *What is the target market (geography, size, industry)?*

The target market should be clearly identified. This is often achieved by geography and company size. At PayMaxx, we started by presenting our services in middle Tennessee to employers with 100-1000 employees. We have since expanded this range and geography to encompass customers with 1-10,000 employees nationwide. Your geography and size may be different. It could be the city where you live or a few counties or your state. Whatever your geography is, make sure you have the resources to cover (flood) it. Do not start by attempting to be a national company. You will likely fail. Also, narrowing your market by targeting a certain size customer and further narrowing it by a few specific industries will certainly enhance your chances of success. The key points here are to narrow your scope and have a clearly defined target.

❑ *How do we reach them (list, push/pull marketing)?*

Now that you have a scope and target market clearly defined, you must find a way   of reaching those prospects that fit the criteria. You must fiercely avoid breaking out of your target market. If Tennessee is your market and a prospect calls from California, you should think long and hard before taking the purchase order. If you're smart and in the early stages of your development, you will turn that person down.

You can also buy lists from trade associations, Dun & Bradstreet, online yellow pages, or any other list providers. Buy the list, and then decide on a tactic to reach your target audience. Direct mail is useful in the business services arena if followed up with telemarketing. Send them a postcard and then call them. If you have the resources and manpower, you can use pull-marketing techniques, such as advertising, trade shows, and so on.

❏ *What is the hook (an aspect of your differentiation)?*

You have narrowed the field; you have devised a plan to reach the target audience. What is your hook, once you reach your prospect? It has to be an aspect of your differentiation. It is imperative that your hook be limited to *only one* aspect of your differentiation, not a list! Pick the most important or the most dramatic aspect. Too many items will only confuse the customer. This hook should be important enough to the customer that he gives you an appointment to make your pitch.

During the early years at PayMaxx, our hook was our fixed-fee billing structure. We also guaranteed satisfaction: If a customer did not like our service, we would pay the expense for them to go back to their previous provider or elsewhere. This offer, exuding self-confidence, turned many, many heads.

❏ *What is the pitch (your value proposition)?*

You're in the door. You have 15 minutes. What is your pitch? The perfect pitch is a crisp, well-rehearsed four-step presentation designed to overcome the four mental blocks (obstacles) that any potential customer subconsciously places in front of you. These are *"No Trust," "No Need," "No Help,"* and *"No Hurry."* In this exact order, you must overcome these obstacles.

First, the customer does not *trust* you. So begin the pitch by telling him who you are and how long you have been in business. Drop the names of your happy customers and any awards or recognitions you may have won.

Second, the customer has no *need*. You must quickly establish why he needs your product. He'll save money, improve efficiency, automate a process, etc. So the customer now trusts you and believes he has a need.

Third, the customer doesn't believe *you* can *help* him. You must quickly establish why your product solves his problem and satisfies his need. Three down, one to go: He now trusts you and believes he has a problem you can fix.

Fourth, now he's in no *hurry*. This is when you come in with a special offer: "If you buy before the end of the month, you will get a discount."

The bottom line is that simply getting in front of the customer and starting out with an offer is ineffective. Any and all pitches – on the phone, in person, or in writing – must follow these four steps in that exact order. Do this, and you will see a steady growth of your customer base and top-line revenue.

❏ *What is the goal (numbers and a timeframe)?*

No strategy can succeed without clearly defined and articulated goals. Sales and growth goals must be specific, verifiable, and numerical. They must have timeframes. They must be measurable. You have to associate these goals with your revenue drivers. Track them, chart them, and communicate them. *Remember: If you are not measuring anything, you are not managing anything.* Successful, growing enterprises have charts and graphs on the walls of every manager's office. This creates enthusiasm in the company and gets people involved.

Putting It All Together

The following graph illustrates the interplay among the fundamental principles associated with sustained growth. It depicts them as layers or floors in a structure.

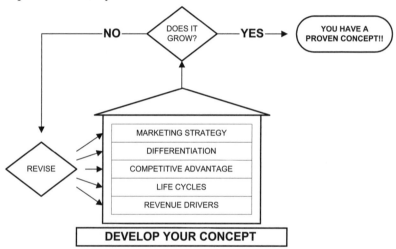

If after several attempts, you do not see any growth, then your concept (your foundation) could be flawed, and you might have to start over.

Sustaining the Momentum

Once you have a proven concept and are experiencing growth, you can't just sit back and expect the growth to continue and the cash to roll in. You must continually analyze and adjust your model, concept, and business metrics to sustain your growth. When you do this regularly and successfully, as a matter of habit, then you will be able to sustain your growth and achieve momentum. To keep that momentum, you must repeat the following four steps over and over again:

❑ *Act:* Take initiative. Make decisions and act on them. Don't sit around worrying too much. Make it happen!

❑ *Measure:* Count it, chart it, and graph it. Do not rely on any uninformed estimates to make strategic or operational decisions. You should quantify all aspects of your company's performance by measuring everything possible.

❑ *Reflect:* Once you have quantified data, you will have something to analyze. Take a long look, and ask yourself if the numbers could be better. The answer will almost always be yes.

❑ *Correct:* Adjust your systems, procedures, or policies so the next round of numbers will look better. Then return to step one and act on them.

These steps, like the spokes of a wheel, must go round and round. The process is never-ending, and you should be relentless in driving your organization to institutionalize it. If you ever tire of this process, either take a sabbatical from your business, or consider retirement.

Challenging the Big Boys

Put a bowling ball and a marble side-by-side on a table. Thump the bowling ball. What happens? Nothing! Then thump the marble with the same force. What happens? It flies across the room! This illustrates that mass and acceleration are inversely proportional. This basic law of physics can be used with brutal effectiveness against your giant competitors. Your small entrepreneurial business can move fast to bring products and services to the market way ahead of your competition.

PayMaxx has always been the innovation leader in the payroll industry. In spite of our size (1:400 compared to the largest player), we introduced the first Windows-based PC payroll outsourcing service in the market. The giant followed nearly two years later with its version. We were the second to offer a comprehensive, Internet-based payroll outsourcing service, in January 1999. The giant followed us a year later. It is ironic that PayMaxx was awarded the prestigious 2001 MVP award for its PowerPayroll.com, while the giant was recognized as the runner-up!

So, do not be intimated by the size of the big boys. Turn their greatest asset – their size – into their greatest liability. Quick turnaround on decisions, rapid customer response, going beyond the call of duty, customizations, and so on are your advantages. Use them. Doing this will turn your greatest liability – your size – into your greatest asset.

Measuring Success

What is success? Is it measured by wealth? Is it based on fame? The fact is that success is situational and varies from person to person. In the final analysis, success is meaningful only in the context of one's vision for the future and personal goals. A violinist with modest economic means and expectations who sets out with his life goal to perform at the Carnegie Hall and eventually achieves it is successful, even though he may not have accumulated any wealth in the process. On the other hand, an entrepreneur who accumulates $25 million by age 40 – considered successful by many – has failed in achieving his own vision of success if his goal was to accumulate $50 million in wealth. So success can be defined by the degree to which one achieves goals and realizes his or her vision. One thing is certain: If you don't measure anything, you won't be successful.

Most young companies are undercapitalized and do not have a huge stream of cash flowing into the business. Nor do they have a client list that's a mile long. They do, however, have a measurable growth curve. As depicted in the *lifecycle,* successful young companies will grow rapidly before they reach maturity and efficiency. The key is to establish quantifiable and achievable goals and measure your performance against those objectives. This way, you will always know whether you are succeeding or failing.

At PayMaxx, we defined the yardstick in our industry to be the number of people employed by our clients (census). Then we began ranking the industry accordingly. Using this yardstick, we are now the 12th largest in our industry. This ranking is out of approximately 1,500 providers. We consider this a great accomplishment and relative success. We have set out to be the 5th largest, so we still have a way to go.

Success is measured in the context of your goals and your vision for the future of your company. If you realize your vision or achieve your goal, then by definition you have succeeded. Of course, your company's vision and goals must be clearly articulated, written, and communicated.

Taking Risk

Let's go to the dictionary (www.dictionary.com) for help on this one!

Entrepreneur: A person who organizes, operates, and *assumes the risk* for a business venture

Enterprise: An undertaking, especially one of some scope, complication, and risk

Risk is intertwined with and inseparable from entrepreneurship. If you cannot accept or take the risk, do not start. I am often amused by would-be entrepreneurs who are stunned that the local bank requires a "personal guarantee" from them to secure a loan for their business. Many do not think twice about signing the guarantee because of the power of their conviction and their belief in their own ability to succeed. Many recoil at the thought of the potential risk and never get started. The key questions you should ask yourself are: "If I do not believe in my business and my ideas, why should the bank? If I am not willing to take risks, why should an investor?" They won't.

Understanding Leadership

I believe many people have a basic misunderstanding about leadership. They simply equate leadership to management, but there is a significant difference. Leaders inspire. They create energy where it did not exist before. They are able to request, and receive, sacrifices from those following them. Leaders raise their followers to higher levels of performance – levels that the followers may not have believed possible. They have a clear vision of the future. They have seen the Promised Land and they take their followers to it.

Leaders also understand the strengths and weaknesses of their followers. Some followers are in need of inspiration, while others are simply in need of direction. Leaders provide both, and this is where leadership and simple management skills part company. Inspiring others is part of the true leader's personality. So, despite much of today's popular "management think," it is my opinion that this ability is innate and cannot be taught. True leaders are born leaders. "Leadership Training" is an oxymoron. This does not mean that a natural leader cannot benefit from training and learn new leadership skills.

In his mid twenties, Alexander the Great, one of the most effective military leaders in the history of mankind, set out from Macedonia to conquer the known world. Ten years later, in 324 B.C., he returned triumphantly. He had vanquished all the great empires, including Greece, Persia, and India. On his way back from India, he took the southern route through the Arabian deserts. A large segment of his army perished in the deserts – what the swords of his enemies could not do, the heat of the sun, the sand storms, and lack of water accomplished. His chronicler records that one night Alexander's servant brought him a bowl of water. Alexander asked his servant, "Have the soldiers had their share?" "No, sire. There is not enough to go around." Alexander refused the water, lamenting, "If my soldiers cannot drink, neither will their commander." This story is a powerful example of the innate qualities that endear leaders to their followers. Alexander did not learn this in a classroom.

The leader's actions – not words alone – endear him or her to the troops. Once that magical relationship is established between the leader and the troops, he or she can then go out and ask them to charge the enemy, put themselves in harm's way, even sacrifice their lives, and they will do so willingly. This quality of leadership can never be taught to someone who does not posses it innately, no matter how many certificates or degrees are displayed on their office walls.

Rules to Live and Grow By

When you have been around for a few years you begin to develop your own set of "golden rules." These are things to avoid and rules to follow. I have developed my own catalogue:

Things to Avoid

Avoid get-rich-quick schemes. They are all false! The principles, elements, and processes described earlier in this chapter cannot be rushed. If you have any doubts, just ponder the vast cemetery of failed dot-coms from the past few years.

Avoid an overly rapid growth rate. You must grow the business in a sustained, methodical manner at a growth rate that the organization, systems, and structure can absorb without being destabilized.

Avoid promising what you cannot deliver. In fact, it is better to underpromise and overdeliver than the other way around. A corollary to this is not to sell futures, such as what you will have, but rather what you already have as a deliverable.

Avoid hunting elephants. This refers to huge customers. Pursue rabbits, squirrels, and deer before going after elephants. Furthermore, do not accept a customer that would constitute more than 10 percent of your total revenues. If you do, be prepared for the tail to wag the dog.

Avoid taking profits out of the company in its first five to 10 years. Pay yourself a decent salary, and keep everything else plowed back in. Capital to growth is like fuel to a race car. Without it, growth and speed will suffer.

Avoid hiring friends and family. There are exceptions to this rule; however, they are so rare and improbable that I think this should be avoided entirely. Having friends and family as employees puts you in a no-win situation. If you reward them, everyone else will believe it is based on the relationship. If you don't, the family member will think you are taking them for granted. Whatever you do, you will eventually lose.

Avoid sloppy accounting. Hire a good accountant. Keep good sets of accounting books and records. Pay your taxes. Stay within the boundaries of the law and regulations. The distraction caused by cutting corners will be far more costly than any short-term gains.

Avoid analysis paralysis. Planning, modeling, budgeting, and consulting are indispensable to sound decision-making. However, at some point you must recognize you've analyzed enough, and it's time to fold or act.

The Golden Rules

- ❑ Articulate a vision; communicate it; chart a path to getting there.
- ❑ Have goals and measurements.

- ❏ Act; measure; reflect; correct. Repeat these four steps forever.
- ❏ Conduct business in an ethical manner.
- ❏ Be fair-minded and just.
- ❏ Have strong opinions without being opinionated. There is a difference.
- ❏ Have enough self-confidence to hire people who are better than you.
- ❏ Believe in yourself and your people.
- ❏ Pursue excellence in all things.
- ❏ Focus. Do not engage in unrelated activity.
- ❏ Balance recurring expense with recurring revenues.
- ❏ Balance the interest of your three key constituents: employees, shareholders, and customers.
- ❏ Genuinely care for the well-being of your employees without being entangled in their lives.
- ❏ Offer and demand respect. Respect is non-negotiable and is given freely until there is reason not to give it. Trust, however, is earned.
- ❏ Earn the trust of your employees and customers.
- ❏ If your employees love you, appreciate it, but do not be in need of it.
- ❏ Keep clean, accurate books and as many operating metrics as you can.
- ❏ Share financial and operating metrics with your employees.
- ❏ Have regular meetings with your senior staff, and expect them to do the same with their teams.
- ❏ Hire good people. Do your best to retain them.
- ❏ Delegate! Set boundaries and get out of their sand boxes.
- ❏ Have a long-term perspective. Avoid short-term solutions.

❏ What you have to do eventually, do immediately.

❏ Share the wealth through stock options and ownership.

❏ Treat your employees the way you want to be treated. If you do not want to get a phone call in the middle of the night, don't call them in the middle of the night. If you want to go home and have dinner with your family, ensure they have the same opportunity.

❏ Avoid Mushroom Management (Keep employees in the dark; feed them manure; they will be happy). This mindset is flawed. Employees must be informed.

❏ Keep your word. Your word must mean more than any written contract.

❏ Do not allow or engage in office politics, favoritism, gossip, or backbiting.

❏ Be a team member while you are the team leader.

❏ Balance constructive criticism with recognition and praise.

❏ Business is not a democracy; it is a benevolent dictatorship. Encourage and receive input, but do not be afraid of imposing your will if it serves the best interest of the enterprise.

❏ Demand excellence. Tolerate mistakes, but punish repeat offenders.

❏ Avoid gold-plating. Good should not become the hostage of perfect.

Farsheed Ferdowsi has been the driving force behind PayMaxx's spirit and commitment to being among the leaders in the employer services industry. Having been in the outsourcing and information technology business for more than 21 years, he is highly regarded for his ability to manage and grow technology-centric service companies, and his hands-on involvement is evident throughout the company.

Mr. Ferdowsi started Access Data in 1979 to develop business software and spun off PayMaxx in 1994 when that department demonstrated potential for rapid growth and success. Aside from the businesses in which he has an interest, he serves on the board of directors for a number of nonprofit and for-profit organizations.

Mr. Ferdowsi holds a master's degree in structural engineering from the University of California at Berkeley and a bachelor's degree in civil engineering from Vanderbilt University.

FROM MOM & POP TO NATIONAL PLAYER

JACK LAVIN
Arrow Financial Services
President and Chief Executive Officer

Starting and Sustaining Momentum

Early in my career I surrounded myself with talented people, a practice which continued into my second career and has served me and our company well. We transformed an entrepreneurial debt collection agency into a 1,000-employee, $60 million accounts receivable management firm with offices throughout the country. My focus has been and will continue to be to direct my business for long-term success, to be a significant participant in the accounts receivable management sector. We will accomplish this by retaining a balanced approach between conservative conduct and opportunistic ideologies. The way we run our company is based on hiring people with different points of view, people who are skilled in what they do and who are not afraid to challenge the system. This creates an environment conducive to excellence through training and truly developing associates, establishing corporate momentum, and offering a dynamic career for all capable employees.

This is a fragmented industry in the midst of ongoing consolidation. We are unique in this industry because our peers are either public entities or are controlled or owned by large private equity firms. At the other end of the spectrum are a multitude of very small agencies servicing smaller, usually local, clients. We are well positioned to take advantage of the numerous opportunities this sector has to offer over the next five to 15 years. It is our intention to leverage our unique position and grow our company smartly and profitably.

Arrow was founded by my father, Robert Lavin, in 1961 and grew profitably under his leadership. My education and experience had provided no training for the challenges associated with working with family members in a family business. It was a challenge to convince them that we had the kernels and elements of an operation that could become a significant participant in the industry. It was even more challenging to persuade my family that we needed to develop a strategy to address imminent industry consolidation to ensure that we were positioned to not only survive but flourish. One specific initiative I suggested was to buy portfolios, rather than service them as agents. Since no capital is at risk when you service delinquent accounts as a contingency agent, it was difficult to persuade my family to purchase portfolios. Ultimately we did buy a few portfolios to see how they would perform. The portfolios performed as my brother Ron suggested they would, which resulted in Arrow entering the portfolio acquisition business.

Once we were convinced that our strategy should embrace both the contingency and purchased portfolio activities, the next challenge was to institutionalize Arrow's infrastructure. Specifically, we needed to establish written policies and procedures relating to documentation, audited financial statements, compliance matters, and human resources, to begin with. This initiative, in many ways, was much more difficult than changing our strategy. Eventually, we decided to take on a partner to help us understand the need for establishing these policies and procedures and, more important, to provide implementation support.

One example of this challenge was related to hiring a treasurer. My two partners understandably focused on the cost and noted that the treasurer would be in a non-revenue-producing position, and for that salary we could hire six or seven account representatives. It took one to two years for me to convince my partners we needed not only accounting/treasury staff, but also technology and human resources to support our strategic plan. Since they were much more focused on the operations than on strategy, this requirement was less obvious to them than it was to me then. We jointly decided that if we could combine good operators (collection professionals – my partners Ron Lavin and Brian Cutler) and good strategists (me), we would have an edge over most our competition for the next few years. We had either people like me – an ivory-tower, suit-wearing guy who does not like to dirty his hands – or people like my brother, who is a pure operator. If we could combine the two symbiotically, I felt we could truly define synergy and accomplish the growth we desired in the industry.

The Team and the Vision

When communicating our vision and strategy to our clients and potential clients, we stress our stability and commitment. We tell them we have been in business for 40 years and will be here as a mutually beneficial partner for the long term. It will be win-win relationships, because those are the only ones that survive over the long haul. We remain steadfast on creeds of ethics, integrity, and credibility. Internally, we tell our people they are able to create their own career velocity. We tell them we will provide all of the tools they will need to prosper, as well as management consistency. If there is a rule, there is a rule. We want our stability and reliability to be our selling points, both internally and externally. We encourage an open-door policy and attract staff who have a passion for the business and who share that passion with their colleagues.

As a smaller company in the industry, it was very difficult to attract top talent to form an effective team. We knew the caliber of staff we wanted to attract but could not offer the compensation or platform they required. We had to convince them of our strategy and that significant growth opportunities existed for those who joined us as we transformed from an entrepreneurial enterprise to a larger, more institutional platform.

Earlier in my career I had surrounded myself with a team of people who possessed impressive credentials, and we planned to adopt the same philosophy at Arrow. At this stage of our evolution, though, we had to convince people of the merits of our plan and ask them not only to have faith but also to accept lower compensation than they would earn in a more established company. At this point we had neither the capital nor the infrastructural organization to entice them. We ultimately attracted a CFO, a general counsel, and a human resources manager to help build the infrastructure we needed to execute our strategy. They performed all of the non-glamorous but essential tasks in helping us build the company to where it is today. The same principles we adopted back then still govern Arrow today: Empowering the right people and recruiting people with different views from mine.

After the infrastructure was established, we focused on sharing our vision with key middle management and getting their buy-in. We needed to convince them that our vision was realistic and achievable. We wanted people who agreed with the broad vision but also challenged it if they had a strong, supportable view that certain aspects were unrealistic. We wanted people who would challenge the system and think "outside the box." We spent a considerable amount of time, and still do, cultivating relationships between departments and key staff. We strive to balance internal advancement with the benefits of attracting people with new philosophies from other companies and industries.

The ongoing exercise of transforming Arrow from the "mom and pop" level to a significant national participant demanded that we assemble the right team and establish a sound decision-making process. We are extremely conservative, but we knew we had to take the risks of investing today to be competitive over the long term, even though the breakeven period could be as long as one to two years.

Because of the nature of this industry, we devoted considerable resources to developing a sophisticated underwriting, valuation, and pricing model as it related to purchasing the delinquent portfolios. Thus, when we purchased charged-off portfolios, generally we purchased them for 1 to 20 cents on the dollar. We were one of the pioneers in developing a sophisticated pricing model, which in turn allowed us to be the only company in this sector that did successful securitizations. At that time not many firms would buy these portfolios because of the associated risk and the difficulty in assessing their value. Our main objective was to buy portfolios that we expected to meet our three-year return parameters and forecasts.

One main aspect of this business is the necessity to be able to balance inventory and resources at any moment in time – the volume of paper we buy with the people we have calling and collecting. If you have the correct formula, you can have innumerable people doing this, but you need to have the correct amount of inventory, as well. In the early stages we balanced the purchasing of inventory with our ability to increase the number of collectors in our single Chicago office. We then looked at what it would take to expand by opening new call centers. The first new site was opened in Wisconsin, two hours from our home office. The formula there was the same as everywhere else. We start with a capable manager who embraces and exemplifies the company's vision, and then make sure that he or she is paid well to do well. This manager must have a personal stake and investment in the business. We provide the guidelines for hiring and training.

My management style is collaborative, but the buck stops with me. I make the final decisions, aided by input from involved parties. I make a decision only if the experts and I are on the same page philosophically, and I understand the experts completely. I avoid unilateral decisions and always try to make team decisions. I will often defer to my partners and advisors, who are the experts, but I am responsible for the decision, no matter what the outcome. Decisions must be made collaboratively.

My *modus operandi* tends to be to circle the wagons during tough economic times. I tend to take that one extra step in buying new equipment or hiring a new employee when the economy is tight. A down economy does not entirely stifle growth in this industry. In theory, our industry has an inelastic relationship with the economy – which is one of the reasons I was attracted to this industry in the first place. Our view is that our industry, and therefore Arrow, should be relatively insulated from good or bad economic times, all other things being equal.

The top 30 or 40 industry players are always trying to assess how changes in the economy affect the liquidation rates. We strive to be in a position to be responsive to economic shifts as they occur. We want to know as quickly as possible how a change will affect us in our business. We are constantly looking for signs of shifts in the economy that would affect our ability to collect for our clients or for our own portfolios.

As a smaller business, we have many advantages over the larger players. We are nimble; we can make informed, thorough decisions more quickly, and we can partner with others more readily to close a deal. We can also offer our employees a lot more visibility and access to senior management, as well as the opportunity to make a more substantial impact on the company.

As for getting the attention of larger companies for prospective project partnerships, it is imperative to maintain resolute standards of integrity and performance. We must also remain focused on credibility and reputation. We then have to go out and promote ourselves. Because of our momentum and past growth, the large financial institutions feel very comfortable working with us because of our initiative to professionalize ourselves, which elevates us above our smaller competitors. We are recognized as a proven entity that is able to pass all of the vendor tests, qualifying us as one of the important players in the industry.

Innovation and Success

Customer service is key to running a successful business and to sustaining momentum. The correct recipe is usually discovered through trial and error. Our philosophy is that the company needs to be responsive to the needs of the customer; if not for the customer, the company would not exist. The company must invest time, money, and effort to establish an effective customer service department. As each day passes, we learn new things to improve this department. We are continuously refining our customer service approach, which we can do because of our size, infrastructure, and company vision.

We are conservative but actively look to take advantage of opportunities. We must take risks to grow and prosper. We have taken risks and profited; we also have experienced our fair share of mistakes – but we learn from each one. We constantly seek new opportunities, especially when things are tough for our competitors. We are always taking risks. When Arrow enters into a new business venture, we like to think that the chances for success are between 80 percent and 90 percent.

Because risk is necessary, it is crucial to surround yourself with good people. When speaking with an entrepreneur in a smaller company just starting out, I would advise them to first have a clearly mapped goal and an understanding of how it must be attained. Then I would sit down with them and tell them two things: First, I would stress the importance of communicating the vision of the entrepreneur, especially if dealing with family. It is necessary to have the details as to who will do what, where, when, and why, to get off the ground. Second, the ownership must be clearly defined and understood before momentum can be gained.

To be a leader in our industry – or any industry, for that matter – you must combine an understanding of the dynamics of the business with an understanding of what it takes to manage in an industry where there are countless variables, many of them beyond your control. You must know how to respond and react to these variables. It is equally important that the management team is understood and given the proper guidance and support. They must execute the plan and revise it according to external factors.

Teaching a team to innovate and harnessing their talents are difficult. We obviously want our team to come up with new business ideas that offer new and better ways to do things. We challenge and encourage our people to think about what they really like to do in combination with the company's needs. Then we stress the importance of trying their best in every situation and pushing them to always want to climb. We want them to have ambition, to excel and prosper, and this comes from having the right attitude.

I keep my edge by avoiding complacency, which is easy, given the challenges of the industry. I am constantly looking at our competition. I look at the surrounding landscape for future changes, staying close to customers in good and bad times. This is important because it allows you to monitor their thoughts, which can be keys to innovation and predicting trends. Finally, it is important to do what you say you will do. It is also important to invest, invest, and invest – with an infrastructure that will support your goals. These goals – and how they can change – must be understood internally and externally. A company must be built to prosper in the long term, but to do well in the short term. There needs to be a balance between long- and short-term goals. Surrounding yourself with the best mix of people who will challenge and question, and consequently become an integral part of the company's decision-making process, is key to gaining momentum in an industry and becoming and remaining successful.

In the end, this business, like most others, is largely a function of people. Our success has been a function of our people since my dad started the business in 1960. We try to create a humble environment and never forget how we achieved our goals – having the right people at the right place at the right time. We understand that our staff has personal lives and family, and we encourage a good balance between their personal lives and professional lives. We sincerely attempt to reward achievement and recognize effort in more ways than just dollars. And we continue to try to reduce bureaucracy.

Since 1995 Jack Lavin has contributed to Arrow Financial Services LLC by bringing a wealth of experience from the U.S. and international capital markets, as well as seasoned general management experience.

Mr. Lavin has been very successful in growing and running a number of financial- and consulting-related businesses. He has had extensive experience in developing and implementing business plans, determining policies and strategies, and recruiting and training new and experienced hires. Mr. Lavin spent seven years at Citibank in New York and London, where he served as the head of its European treasury-consulting group for two years. During his three years at Drexel Burnham Lambert, he established and built the International Capital Markets Group, with representation in New York, London, and Tokyo. While at Bankers Trust, he managed the derivative, capital markets and corporate finance business units in New York, London, and Chicago.

Currently Arrow's President and CEO, Mr. Lavin devotes his time to overseeing day-to-day operations and implementing the strategic goals set forth by the company.

Mr. Lavin earned his bachelor's degree from the University of Wisconsin-Madison in 1976 and a master's in International

Management from the American Graduate School of International Management (Thunderbird) in 1978.

TORPEDOES ABOUND! WHY IT'S BETTER TO BE A PT BOAT THAN A BATTLESHIP

Lucinda Duncalfe Holt
Destiny
President and Chief Executive Officer

On Leadership

The job of leading an emerging growth company requires a unique mix of skills and attributes. I think it is the most fun you can get paid for, but it is also demanding work. The critical elements of success include setting a clear vision, recruiting a team that shares that vision, and managing the activities of the organization. To achieve these, you need a broad mix of skills and attributes.

The basic attribute that all entrepreneurs share is optimism: You have to believe in your vision despite all of the people who tell you you're crazy – and they will. That optimism has to be paired with drive and tenacity that push through the inevitable setbacks. Many great entrepreneurs also have a charisma that draws people toward them and their vision.

Drawing people to the new company is an absolutely critical ability. Early on, when you have nothing to offer but a dream, you have to be able to build a team, interest investors, and sign up clients. That is why sales are such a critical aspect of leading an entrepreneurial company. Selling is what I do about 80 percent of every day.

In addition to selling, general management skills are in the standard tool kit for CEOs. You have to be a quick study, able to learn the areas you haven't managed yourself. You have to be willing to ask really dumb questions in those areas where you lack familiarity. I have always been a jack-of-all-trades-master-of-none, inch-deep-mile-wide type. As a CEO, that becomes a strength; whereas, earlier in your career it could have been a weakness. Despite the wide range of experiences I brought to the job, and an MBA with a number of finance and accounting courses, I was very weak in those areas. By hiring the best outside advisors money could buy (even though we actually did not have enough to pay them at that time) and being willing to ask any question, I learned. It's great if you have a capability, but if you don't, buy or build it. With this set of basic attributes and skill sets, you have a strong foundation to build true leadership.

You will have to define leadership for yourself. After many years of reading on the subject, I have come to the conclusion that there is no standard definition, and that part of becoming a leader is to define it yourself. For me, leadership is about wanting to be the one with the ball when the game is close, and having others want to give you the ball. It takes a certain drive and willingness to step up.

Once you've established your philosophy of leadership, and you are in the leadership role, the specific skills of managing the enterprise should be used in a way that supports your leadership style. Although I have a strong and somewhat unusual belief in how companies should be managed, I think that consistency is more important than anything else. I would have been miserable working for Ross Perot in the early days at EDS, but Ross's management of the company was completely consistent, and it worked. Leadership styles grow directly out of who we are as people, so the better you understand yourself, the better you'll be able to lead.

In terms of management style, Destiny is a highly collaborative company. My management style is very open, empowering, and involving. We share almost all information openly with the whole company (the only exceptions are personnel issues and contractually prohibited communications). Openness is built into the fabric of the organization in many ways. Most important, we have a completely open floor plan, where everyone sits in a low-walled cubicle. That way, everyone can see and hear everything that's going on. We have weekly company-wide meetings, where we share financial information, client updates, and other company news. Our intranet allows anyone to post any news that they think will interest others. I hold office hours every week, when anyone can come to talk with me about anything. Employees frequently spearhead brown-bag lunch sessions to discuss market or technical topics. This foundation of open communication allows us to build many layers of important management structures.

For example, it is hugely important to encourage innovation and to honor the talents of your employees. Failure is a natural byproduct of risk-taking and innovation. You definitely do not want to reward failure, but at the same time, you don't want to punish it, or people won't put themselves in the position to take those risks. You must then create an environment where people are encouraged to innovate, and if you have the right people, they simply will.

As a leader you must be able to empower your executives and middle managers. This is essential for morale, as well as the culture within your firm. Many entrepreneurs are very controlling. They want to own every piece of everything. They want to review every piece of marketing material. They want to build the Web site and write it all themselves. That is a huge drain that will inevitably stunt the growth of the firm. Instead, you must empower people. You must give them something they own, and then you actually have to let them work on it. This is easy when they are working in the same way you would; however, it gets hard when they do something differently than you would. As a leader you have to know when it's is imperative to step in, and when you can give them their own leeway.

Your team must be ready for change. They must enjoy constantly looking at new things. Then you need to focus on developing core capabilities and core attributes that underlie your ability to deal with new technologies and new markets. At the same time, however, you also want to have established expertise in the markets you are addressing. The trick is to create a culture where change is a good thing, where risk is an accepted part of the game, and where failure is something you learn from, not something to be punished. If you do that, and if you have the right people, they will like the environment. They will like a new challenge.

That brings us back to selling. Possibly the most important part of managing a business is finding the right people to join your team. But it's not easy. Essentially, you have to sell the dream. People don't join start-ups for the money. They do it for the journey, for the experience, and because they actually believe in the end goal. Finding people who are willing to do that is hard because typically they will take large pay cuts now for the prospect that they will make money someday in the future. Finding the kind of person who wants to do that is difficult. Every community has entrepreneurial groups, but the most common way of finding the right people comes through networking via friends, family, boards of directors, and advisory boards. For some people, joining a start-up is making a difference in the world. It lights their fire. They are the people you want on your team.

If you have the right team, and you can lead them effectively toward the right vision, you'll have a winner!

Finally, because being a better leader is about being a better human being, a word about integrating real life with work is necessary. The magazines would all have you believe you should be "balanced." For me, it is less about balancing work and family than it is about learning how to blend the two together. I regularly cut out of work during the day to see my daughter, but I also regularly work at home. You have to take the freedom you get as an entrepreneur and use it to carve out a life with your family.

Gaining Traction

Nothing happens in a new business unless you can figure out how to make something out of nothing – how to gain traction. The model we use, which seems to work and is repeatable, is to involve early clients in a win/win relationship. You have to focus on one key client and create a value proposition for them that is compelling and unique to your company. If your vision is right, you will be able to offer something no one else can. Since you are creating a win for the customer, they will be happy to create a win for you. For example, they may fund product development for you, refer your next customer, or support your marketing efforts. Those early customers can become your most vocal and useful advocates. Note that you are not focused on revenue or profits with these early clients, but are looking for leverage points that will turn that one customer into 10.

One of the most important uses for those early advocates is to help you gain buzz within your community, whether that community is geographic-, industry-, or client-oriented. Buzz can help you establish credibility when looking for outside funding, hiring early employees, and signing more customers. With a carefully defined target market, you can create valuable awareness with a press campaign that focuses on small regional and industry publications. Even though you are a tiny company, if you are cutting-edge, these publications will be interested. In print, or at a podium, your company can appear much larger than it actually is – especially with the support of that early customer – to help you land that next client. It is essential, though, that you have a clear strategy that underlies the buzz you create.

One of the common mistakes companies made during the dot-com era was creating lots of buzz about a business model that didn't work. Two key books can help at this stage: Geoffrey Moore's *Crossing the Chasm* and Jay Levinson's *Guerrilla Marketing*. The former lays out some very basic, but extraordinarily useful ideas about how to think about products and marketing in new markets, and the latter provides great tactical marketing approaches.

We have an approach to getting traction in a market called MicroVertical marketing, which is based on some of Moore's ideas; however, it extends them downward. The basic idea is to define markets very, very tightly, establishing a new level of expertise, thereby changing the rules of the competitive game. For example, most of our competitors look at all of financial services as a single industry, while we look at it as more than 50 industries. So, while our competitors are targeting *American Banker,* we are targeting tiny publications, such as *Private Asset Management.* This allows us to get far more coverage, very cost effectively. It also positions us as an industry insider, which helps drive sales. Finally, we are fighting in much smaller markets, which are sized to our company, while the big boys battle for the big industries. It is critical in this model that you understand how to move from one tiny market to the next; otherwise, you'll be stuck as a tiny company in a tiny market.

Although strategy and marketing are important, nothing in a business is as important as selling. All of the businesses I have been involved with provide products or services to other businesses, and all have used a direct sales force to sell to relatively large clients. Getting traction and growing the business are mainly about getting on the telephone and using your networks to find customers. Early on, no matter what the structure of your company is, you can use a board of directors or an advisory board to help you develop business. You should put people within the industry on your board with the explicit goal of mining their networks for early accounts. Many CEOs get diverted from a primary focus on sales because there is so much else going on, and there are so few people to do the work. This is the single biggest mistake you can make.

But you will have a lot happening. You will spend an inordinately large amount of time worrying about, looking for, and managing money. During the dot-com boom, this is almost all CEOs did. Traditionally, "bootstrapping," or building the business from within, was how you got started. I think that we're back to that model because valuations from venture capitalists have returned to normalcy. You obviously should try to live on as little outside capital as possible to maintain ownership of your company. You should always take the money you need; a very common cause of failure in venture-backed firms is undercapitalization. So it is essential that you find creative ways to reduce the amount of money you need and to push your need for money as late as possible, when your valuation will be higher. The single best tactic is to get an early customer who supports your growth.

Bootstrapping seems to take a lot longer than getting big venture capital and running flat-out does, but it can be better for the business in the long run. Unless there are very real, competitive, time-to-market pressures, you may be better off managing against reasonable timeframes. ("Reasonable" in startup terms – not in large corporate terms. You still have to run a hundred miles an hour!) Venture capitalists say it takes twice as long and costs twice as much as you think to get a business off the ground, and they're right. During the dot-com boom, we managed very conservatively. Many people cast aspersions on our approach, saying we were being too conservative. We didn't have the kind of hit that some other firms did, but at the same time, we didn't suffer the downfalls other firms did. Trying to run too fast may leave you falling flat on your face. An idea is very important, but three-quarters of success is based on execution. This is not to say your company should go slowly and steadily, but setting a reasonable pace is important.

A company should not avoid risk altogether, though. On the contrary, taking risk is critical. The key is to understand where the equation is unfair to your advantage and take those risks. I want to enter the market where I think I have an unbalanced competitive advantage. If someone else has the competitive advantage, I don't want to go there. The whole trick with risk is to look at it coldly, without emotion, finding the imbalances, and take those risks that are tipped in your favor.

On Venture Capital

Every venture capitalist has an agenda, but the good ones recognize they will be successful only when the entrepreneur is successful. It is very difficult to figure out what kind of venture capitalist you're negotiating with. You should certainly get references from former portfolio companies. You want references from big successes, but also from failures. How venture capitalists have handled themselves in a failing situation can tell you a lot about them. Venture capitalists will always give you references they think will be good, so try to find out who they have invested in before and call them directly. You may get a different story. You should also talk with the attorneys, accountants, and others who work with many venture capitalists about their reputation.

In the courtship dance with a venture capitalist, there is nothing wrong with trying to extract value from them during the process, whether or not you actually end up taking their money. Their behavior will tell you what they will be like as partners in your business. For example, can they make introductions for you? If they can't do it for you before you take the money, there is no magic that will make them to do it afterward. Test them in the process.

Over the span of your entire life, you will do as many deals as the venture capitalists may do in a year. Because of this, when dealing with venture capital, you must make sure you hire terrific advisors. When it comes to attorneys and accountants, cost should never be an issue. They have done even more deals than the venture capitalists. The right team can help you avoid the many pitfalls. A side benefit to hiring the big-name advisors is that it signals the venture community that you know the game, which gives them more confidence in you.

One of the biggest issues entrepreneurs have when dealing with venture capital is less about legalities than it is about attitude. When you start out, you have nothing but optimism. You are sure and confident, not even thinking about what will happen in a deal if things go wrong. The reality is that almost all venture-backed companies face real challenges along their way to success. There will be ugly times, and preparation for those times is critical. You must know specifically what will happen when things turn downward, attitudinally, as well as legally. For example, when you are going through the deal structure, you must understand what happens in the event of liquidation or in a sale for less than the current valuation or how you can get fired. I remember cutting my first couple of venture deals and thinking, "Who cares about preferences in liquidation? That will never happen," and, "The taxes won't matter when I have that much money." But I have come to care about both of those things! Your attorney, if he's good, will explain all of this, but it's up to you to listen and appreciate its importance.

In addition to selecting the right backers and doing the right deal, thinking about the strategic mix of investors is key. Our company has successfully put together a slate of venture capitalists, so we not only gain more expertise and insight, but we also dilute the power of each. Negotiating who has board seats and who has the rights to name outside directors can be important. You may also be able add some strategic investors into the mix. There are many tactics in this area, and it doesn't matter, ultimately, which ones you use, but you should think about the area strategically.

Entrepreneurial momentum is an amazing force that takes over a firm. It is built drop by drop by a series of small events. Early customers lead to angel investors, who introduce you to more customers. Those customers may drive strategic relationships that provide key support in raising venture capital. If you orchestrate these events, a real momentum can build and potentially sustain your company through the early days.

Momentum can also work against you – when things start to slide, they can go very quickly! The critical point is to manage your cash. As long as you have cash, you're okay, but without it, all the momentum in the world won't help. It is difficult to walk the tightrope between retaining equity and having comfortable cash.

Gaining entrepreneurial momentum does not change significantly over time. The business is fundamentally the same as it was 100 years ago. We had an odd bubble during the dot-com boom, where all of a sudden everyone could make a billion dollars doing just what four others had already done, but doing it with more money. I don't think that is fundamentally value creating, which showed out in the market place. Entrepreneurial momentum is about choosing the right spot, working hard and being lucky.

On Measuring Success in a Small Business

As a new or smaller business, you can do a lot that our big competitors can't. One of our clients once said he had plenty of battleships around, but he wanted a PT boat. Destiny was that PT boat. The biggest advantage you have is agility because you can spot trends early. You can play in much riskier water. You like to be in the choppy part of the wave, on the very edge, just as it's curling over, with the big companies all behind you because it's

159

just too risky for them. If you can create an ability to reliably catch those waves and to be comfortable there, that is a sustainable competitive advantage.

Another advantage for a small company is the ability to define, and own, very small markets. For you, a market of $100 million or $500 million is a good-size market. For the big companies, that's meaningless, so they won't compete with you there. Carving out that kind of niche is all about focus. I believe that in entrepreneurial environments, focus is everything. There are always opportunities around. The trick is to pick the right opportunity and focus on it. If you picked the wrong one, change. Many companies try to do everything at once and do nothing more than trip and fall.

So how do you pick the one? The first thing you must do is get reliable market data, and the only way to do that is by being in the market. Reading an industry report won't do it. You must talk to customers in the market, and once you think you have found a thread, you must basically define the market around that thread of interest and align everything you do around that thread. After a couple of months, if your idea just isn't working, start over. Don't keep working on something that just isn't right.

Success is then measured over multiple dimensions. First and foremost is measuring success in terms of return to the shareholder. As a private company, success is not so much about the specifics of profitability or revenue growth as it is about enterprise value. Have you in fact created value for your shareholders? We know when we are creating value, partially based on the financial metrics of the firm, but also based on the external market. We are being judged not only on how well we are performing in comparison to our peer groups, but also on whether we chose the right peer group; that is, have we picked the right market in which to compete? Our employees and our clients measure the success of Destiny. Are we giving our employees interesting work? Are they enjoying their work? Are we delivering what our clients want and need? For us, customer service is about an entire team of people working directly with a customer. It is doing the right thing. If you live by the Golden Rule, customer service, in a way, doesn't need to exist. Instead, it is more about a partnership of you and your client working toward a specific goal. It is important to realize business is just people working with people. A boss first gave me this piece of advice early in my career, and he was absolutely right. It is so easy to get caught up in what products and feature sets you are building, but if you don't have the people side of it right, fundamentally, nothing else matters. If we do these things, the rest tends to take care of itself.

In fact, the Golden Rule of business is really the direct corollary of the true Golden Rule. People tend to think of business as win/lose. I believe win/win, or 1+1=3, is the real basis of business. If you approach things from the fundamental worldview that a good transaction is good for everyone, you will build value for yourself and everyone with whom you work. That will create a positive reinforcing cycle that you'll benefit from continuously.

Lucinda Duncalfe Holt is president and chief executive officer of Destiny, overseeing its management team and providing strategic direction to the organization. Under her guidance, Destiny has developed a concentrated expertise in financial services, which has led to working successfully with clients such as Citigroup, Mellon, UBS PaineWebber, and the Northern Trust Company. In the six years since Ms. Holt joined Destiny, revenues have increased dramatically, and the company has continued to be positioned for growth. Last year, Inc. *magazine named Destiny the 32nd fastest-growing privately held company in America on its annual Inc. 500 list.*

Ms. Holt has spent her career in financial services, at American Express and SEI Investments, and with startups, including ACP and Infonautics. She graduated cum laude *from the University of Pennsylvania and earned an MBA from the Wharton School.*

LESSONS LEARNED ALONG THE WAY

ART FEIERMAN
Presenting Solutions
Founder and Chief Executive Officer

From the Garage…

I learned something useful even before I launched my company in the garage.

In the early 1980s I had the opportunity to join a startup company called Presentation Technologies. Leaving a somewhat cushy job with Epson America as a major accounts sales manager, I believed Presentation Technologies looked like too good an opportunity to pass. As the story was told, six of the larger venture capital firms in Northern California, including Mayfield, had created an early incubator named Onset, but with a twist. And here lies my starting point. When I was offered a position, it was explained this way:

VC (venture capital) money has mostly been invested in small companies headed by creative, forward-thinking entrepreneurs. Unfortunately, entrepreneurs have their limitations. They may be great at ideas and running small businesses, but most lack the skills to grow a company past a certain point. To make matters worse, as venture capital is provided, the VC team does not gain enough control to guide the company's growth. They can recommend and influence, but majority control remains typically with the founder. As a result, much that needs to be done, such as building infrastructure, solid process, and execution, and developing a forward-thinking and well-mapped plan to be a larger-size company, tend to come up short.

So it was Onset's charter to create companies from scratch – with no entrepreneurs. Instead, Onset would do market research to identify high-potential market niches and opportunities. Once a potential market was discovered, they would do further research, develop a strategy to attack that market, and then *build* a company from scratch, with a top-flight management team, armed with the research and sufficient capital to become a fast-growing, successful company.

From this I drew Lesson #1: Entrepreneurs just don't know when to quit; or, rather, entrepreneurs often fail to recognize when they are out of their depth.

Armed with this valuable lesson imprinted on my brain, fewer than three years later I launched my own company out of a spare bedroom and a garage. (You have to start in your garage to be successful don't you?)

In fact, if you happen to be the president of your company, it might just be interesting to step back and assess the skills and experience you would want to find in a company president if you were looking for someone to replace yourself. Then consider your own skill sets and knowledge. Would you hire yourself to be your next company president – to lead your company in further growth?

Now, back to the tale of Onset and Presentation Technologies: At the time this was happening (1984–86), desktop publishing was all the rage, and Presentation Technologies was created to go after a related market – desktop presentations – by designing and marketing a desktop slidemaker that allowed business and researchers to create high-quality 35mm presentation slides in-house for $.50, instead of $25 to $100 per slide from commercial companies.

To make this work, Onset built a powerful management team, including senior executives and sales management from such companies as HP, MIPS, Polaroid, and Sun Micro. That high-powered team and those stock options allowed the company to draw talent like a magnet.

Even the big boys though, can make mistakes. The market potential, according to contracted research, would grow to better than 5,000 of these slide makers a month within five years. At $5,000 apiece, a $300,000,000-a-year opportunity (less with falling prices, but then related products would be identified to further grow the company), and with more than $19 million in VC money in three years, the company was poised to dominate. Alas! It took 10 years for the market to surpass 500 units a month, and in fewer than three years, the VCs pulled the plug. The company shrank from more than 100 employees to a handful over the next year. Thus ended a dream for many, and it left us with lots of stock options good only for wallpaper.

So there I was, painfully unemployed, following Presentation Technologies' downsizing. In briefly testing the market, I found no inspiring positions, so, like my parents before me, I decided to be the entrepreneur, launching Presenting Solutions (PS) as a reseller of presentation products. I immediately signed up to sell the products from my old company, but did something my competition (mostly small companies of one to five people) wasn't doing: I decided to sell more than one brand. By adding the other brands (by then there were five), I could offer customers a choice: "I don't really care which system you buy – as long as, first, you are truly satisfied, and second, you refer your colleagues to me."

This simple differentiator in my market niche allowed the company to do well. As it grew, my wife, Lori, joined the company full time, adding her organizational skills to my creative skills; we made a good team.

Lesson #2: Look at the competition. See what they are doing well, but more important, identify what they're not doing – that's often where the opportunities lie.

Disruptive Technologies: A Good Head Start

What is a disruptive technology? Consider it a broad term that indicates something new that can change the way companies do business. It can be an idea, a technology, or a process. It could be said that the decision to market multiple brands in my market niche was a disruptive technology – that is, a new, different approach. It certainly put the competition at a disadvantage. We were more credible; others sold one brand, which could be the best or the worst at meeting the customer's requirements. Of course, it didn't take long for the competition to adapt and add additional product lines.

Lesson #3: The problem with disruptive technologies is that those "technologies" are disruptive for only a short time. If they prove successful, they are quickly adapted by others and become mainstays.

The big opportunities to turn PS into a growing company started in 1994. From a technology standpoint, the portable LCD projector was born. Far more robust than the LCD panels before it, it opened a huge potential market, and we were ready to run with it. But how fast can you run when you are still essentially a two-person company?

That brings us to the most major disruptive technology of the past 20 years – the launch of the World Wide Web. Until 1994 the text-only world of the Internet had only minor impact on the way the world did business, but the Web changed it all. As a hardcore science fiction reader, when the Web launched, I was already armed with some excellent perspectives of the potential and was ready to run with it.

Here I'd like to recommend two books: *Earth* by David Brin, an amazing work from 1991 that does a startling job of describing much of what the Web looks like today and its impact on the world. A second book, *Snow Crash* by Neal Stephenson, provides insight into the "immersive" potential of the Web.

Back to business now. Projectors became the product we needed to grow our business beyond a tiny niche, but it was the Web that offered the mechanism for rapid growth. So in the second half of 1994 I started writing content for our first Web site, and in February 1995 we launched it with about 80 pages of content, covering the products we sold, lots of in-depth information on how to choose the right product, and to complement all of that, a huge article on how to be a more successful presenter.

There may not have been very many people using the Web that first year, but for all practical purposes, in our market, we had it all to ourselves. And business grew. It took the competition more than two years to make us feel them online, and by that time we had grown the business more than four-fold. It was 1998 before there was any real competitive threat online from the large AV dealers in our industry, and we had grown from roughly $700,000 in 1995 to over $8 million in 1998. But the competition entered with a vengeance, ending PS's annual triple-digit growth.

The Internet – especially the Web – may be the major disruptive technology influencing business over the past seven years, and it continues to evolve, but the primary disruption we were able to use – a new, low-cost marketing tool to reach existing and new markets – is now old. Almost everyone has a Web site; certainly so many of our competitors do that our company – once unique, thanks to the Web, now looks to many as just another company marketing online.

Lesson #4: You must do more than just recognize those paradigm shifts that directly impact your business plan. You have to rethink your plan and adapt to the changes.

Little Fish, Big Fish: Economies of Scale

At PS, we recognized the rapid rise of online competition from our larger competitors, and in many ways we adapted tactically, but often failed to adapt strategically. Here were our focuses:

❑ Rapid growth – obtaining economies of scale for purchasing
❑ Expanded product lines within our segment
❑ Diversification – expanding into new complementary markets

We recognized from the start that we needed to grow rapidly. As resellers, we needed economies of scale – more buying power so we could remain competitive. For the past seven years, that had been a top priority. In 1995 company size for "critical mass" was about $12 million to $15 million to buy at best price, but by mid-2001, that number had quadrupled. While PS grew almost 20 times in that period, we found ourselves far short of where we needed to be to buy right as the market shifted. For the first time that became critical – our industry shifted from a seller-driven model (between manufacturers and dealers), to a buyer's model. Product gluts appeared, and many panicky manufacturers did what they had to, dumping product aggressively in multihundred-unit quantities, a scale too big for PS to play at. As a result, the one- to three-point point advantage our larger competitors had often enjoyed quickly swelled to 10 points, or more in many cases, dramatically curtailing our margins. At the same time, in our industry the "backend dollars" shrank, further reducing margins. This cycle can be found in many manufacturer-distribution models, so watch out. We recognized in late 2000 that the market was shifting to a buyer's model – much to our chagrin.

Lesson #5: You need to do more than just recognize potential shifts in the marketplace; you must assess the impact on your company and take appropriate, definitive action to overcome potential negative impact.

As a reseller, to try to satisfy customer needs, we expanded our product lines over the years as quickly as we could. Instead of three major brands, we grew to 11 at our peak, and this became an obvious mistake. While it allowed us some incremental business, we sacrificed some of the buying power we sorely needed for our top three or four vendors. Worse, our model did not function well with all those competing product lines. The 80/20 rule was in effect: 80 percent of our revenue was coming from just a few products; in fact, all those extra major brands never generated more than 15 percent of our revenue at best, and had we not had them, we could still have captured over half of that business.

In exchange for taking on those extra lines, we found ourselves with longer inventory turns, often taking significant hits to our bottom line as slow-moving inventory sat around well after manufacturer price protection ran out, forcing us to sell off too much product at a loss or insignificant profit. While some of that is always bound to happen, we found ourselves taking far too many huge hits that could have been avoided with more control and fewer product lines. This was a true lose/lose: lower margins and higher costs.

Lesson #6: You can't please all the people all the time. Although we had good intentions, trying to please all potential customers can be very expensive and not in the best interest of the company.

So we increased our market reach by diversification. With a primary model of marketing over the Web (with some print) and driving prospects to our Web sites and then to the phones, we also maintained a small field sales force. It was easy to recognize that we needed to expand beyond projector sales. We would find a customer, sell a projector, and then have nothing else to sell them but accessories. Recognizing this shortcoming, we looked at and started selling plasma displays, video conferencing, and Web-based conferencing.

Lesson #7: Your competition's mistakes can be your downfall. It's up to you to prevent it.

Sound strange? But it can be true. Here's what I learned.

By 1998 and early 1999, all the big boys in our industry (inspired, I like to think, by our success) felt a burning obligation to jump into the Internet with the enthusiasm of the Airborne jumping out of planes. And many of them got caught in dot-com fever. Internet at any cost! Our finely balanced online advertising and promotion strategy took serious damage, as some competitors – having no concept except "I have to be visible on the Web at any cost" – completely disrupted advertising costs by bidding up the cost of almost every conceivable advertising option.

This disruption had an impact on virtually every industry out there, and the AV industry was no exception. In less than two years, CPM (cost per minute) for highly targeted advertising in our industry surged three to five times, and at the same time, the quality was rapidly diluted. In 1997–98, when buying a banner to advertise on search engines, you were the only advertising on that search engine page. By last year there were typically six to 12 advertisers on one page – some banners, some skyscrapers, some text links. As a result, everyone was paying far more and getting far less.

In our own experience, "click-thru" (the number of people clicking to go to your Web site) rates dropped by 70 percent to 80 percent while the cost more than doubled. In the past couple of years the CPC (cost per click) model emerged, so companies can pay based on delivered traffic instead of mere visibility, but even this didn't help. With some sites using bid-for-position (highest bid gets top placement), you quickly get a good picture of your costs. In our industry for example, words like "LCD projector" surged to $14 to deliver one person to our Web site. And this is my point. These numbers were run up by competitors caught in the fever – no analysis – for at $14 per click, it might well cost $1,000 to acquire enough customers to make one sale that generates only $400 in gross profit (GP). Now there's a tough way to make a living.

Of course, the foolish learned quickly, and today those $14 CPCs are back down in the $2 and $3 range. Even that is still way too high for most companies to make a living in our industry. It is not surprising that perhaps the two biggest bidders – the folks keeping the prices that high – are newcomers to our industry – Dell Computer and Office Depot. Perhaps they are willing to take the hit to build market share or are just caught up in the game. Or, because of their brand identities, maybe they can actually turn a profit with those otherwise high marketing costs.

Lesson #8: It's the execution, dummy!

Perhaps the single most important lesson learned is that you can have all the market savvy you would want and come up with great ideas, but *unless you can execute efficiently in a timely manner, the rest won't do you much good.*

The huge timeline advantage PS had in getting online allowed for plenty of trial and error, but my entrepreneurial style was always "shoot from the hip." That is, take an idea, throw it out, and hope it worked. Far too often perfectly good ideas were launched without any real plan. The results were pretty consistent. Ideas that should have been executed smoothly and cost effectively in a month or two, but lacked any real process and execution, took many months, were often plagued with mistakes and lack of focus, and ultimately failed.

The Cure for the Common Entrepreneur

Not living in a complete vacuum, I knew I needed to surround myself with others who could help grow the company. That can take the form of internal management or outside consultants or coaches – an "executive team" that meets regularly to assess strengths, weaknesses, opportunities, and execution.

What I have learned here could fill many chapters. Here are a few really good lessons.

I needed to know how to continue to grow the business. To keep things lean, I had a marketing company on retainer and another for PR. We also relied on a "rent-a-CFO" to oversee the financial side. They brought me a business plan consultant and ultimately an executive coach. And for the first time, I had a team.

One thing I was told repeatedly was, "As you grow your company, you have to learn to delegate to others." Now there was one piece of advice that really made sense, and one that is often hard for entrepreneurs to follow. I think, as a group, we tend to be very hands-on.

About two years ago I brought in a general manager and started delegating some marketing and advertising decisions to our marketing coordinator and to our outside consultants. I let my accounting manager plan to convert to a more robust accounting package. The pace definitely picked up, as I was out of the loop for many decisions, even though I was needed to sign final documents for most decisions.

Sound great? Not a chance. Either I wasn't listening, or my advisors failed to complete this paragraph: "Art, you have to learn to delegate. You can't micro-manage everything. There's too much going on, and you end up being the bottleneck!"

That's what I heard. Here is the critical missing half:

"Remember, though – delegating doesn't release you from responsibility. Ultimately you need to be sure to set up proper oversight!"

And that is a major league lesson – one that cost our company a heavy toll in wasted money, wasted resources, and lack of focused direction.

Lesson #9: Delegating without proper oversight exposes your company to major potential problems, including loss of cohesive planning, loss of control of costs, and people working at cross purposes.

Lesson #10: Having an executive team and using one effectively are two entirely different matters.

We started having meetings; we looked at our potential future and shaped a vision, but never a process to get there. We even hired a large accounting firm to audit us in case we needed several years of audited returns to go public or, at the least, honest books for potential mergers and acquisitions.

While looking at new markets and directions, I lost some focus on current realities. Advertising costs were soaring, impacting the bottom line, but instead of looking for newer, better methods, I continued to throw more money at what had always worked in the past. My CFO warned me repeatedly that costs were getting out of control, but my response was mostly, "Not a problem, we can cover our higher costs with continued rapid growth." And therein lies the next lesson.

Lesson #11: Getting good advice doesn't help if you don't seriously consider it. You can hang yourself without really trying.

So *pay attention* to the messages you receive from your advisors. Judge them on their merits, not your belief set.

Like many entrepreneurs, I chose to maintain my belief set. I did this by not seriously listening to the advice – I heard but didn't heed. I chose to believe all I had to do was keep growing the business by 30 percent to 50 percent or more a year, and the extra GP would easily keep us profitable while we reached for those important economies of scale I mentioned earlier. After all, for years I plowed as much as 7 percent of the year's revenues (and we're typically working with 20 percent gross profit) into the following year's advertising.

There were many other ideas, suggestions, and warnings, but I tended to gloss over those that weren't convenient.

Building the Team

We grew quickly. My first part-time salesperson helped me with those phone calls coming in from our Web site. He was taking computer courses and ultimately became our IT (information technology) guy. Like the rest of us, he learned as we went. At times, this created problems, but again, we had a huge lead on our competition and were able to execute IT well enough that it didn't become a problem.

In other areas, though, hindsight being 20-20, I should have looked for experienced people instead of "first timers." I hired a general manager with a good background to take over HR, but unseasoned in cost controls, etc. As we searched for a new building, we got carried away. Our building was almost twice as large as we needed; we spent too much on fancy furniture, sophisticated alarm systems, and so on. Ultimately, I was the guy signing on the bottom line, so I'll take the heat, but had I found a seasoned GM, with experience at efficiently running operations, I could have saved the company much money – as much as $150,000 to $180,000 a year in cash flow – and that's just relating to purchasing the new building and accompanying overhead. Other areas where thoughtful spending and cost containment would have fit under a GM role could have saved another $60,000 to $90,000 a year.

Lesson #12: Find the right, experienced people to fill your management team. Learning by trial is a highly overrated and often fatal business strategy.

The "Fundable Executive"

Despite the consultants, I never truly got a handle on how to build a real business plan – I had the ideas but lacked the process to execute. I did latch onto one buzzword I picked up in those venture capital seminars I attended in 1999 during the heyday of dot-com fever: the "fundable executive" – the person to take us to the next level, be it going public, handling a merger or acquisition, or merely growing us into a Fortune 1000 company.

I needed to find that magical, mysterious person with awesome credentials – maybe an ex-IBM exec or someone with much senior management experience, someone who helped take two or three companies public, or into successful mergers or acquisitions.

When we moved to our new building, we even had a large, fully furnished office for our fundable executive.

The only problem was that I had no idea how to find one, nor, other than my description above, what one might look like or what type of fundable executive would fit with our organization. The only real plus I had was my own realization that I have always been a better "idea guy" than a company president. In fact, I always believed that our fundable executive would take the title of president.

Lesson #13: Building the right management team is a process. Like every other aspect of your business, the process, based on well thought out objectives, and once properly defined, needs to be properly executed.

The truth is, we've recently found our fundable executive, but certainly not in the way we anticipated, and not by any intelligent process we created to do so. Still, I believe we finally have the right person to lead us in execution and let us grow our business to the next level.

The Executive Coach

The executive coach is perhaps the most surprising part of my tale because it was totally unlooked for. Through one of the members I was introduced to "my coach." When I first met him, I pointedly asked him what his job description was, and he responded that his job was "to bring joy to my life." Now, that gave me pause, and I could go into many details, but after speaking with him I quickly realized what he could bring to "my party." And in working with him, I also discovered upon meeting many of the people he was also working with, that they were in the midst of major changes in their lives. Most were senior executives of Fortune 500 companies, but at the same time they were looking for new paths and opportunities. He held a weekend retreat, where I met a few of them and learned much about where they had been and where they wanted to be in the future. I certainly had plenty on my plate and wasn't about to leave Presenting Solutions, but I learned many lessons in one short weekend.

One of those I met that weekend is now our company president – and our fundable executive – although it took more than a year for that to happen and very nearly didn't.

Working with a coach has been extremely valuable to me, and I highly recommend it. Of course, like anything else – you need to find the right fit and define your goals and expectations. No, that's not correct: My coach helped me redefine my goals and expectations for running my business and getting the results I desired in business and, to some degree, my personal life, as well.

The Network

Networking in general has never been a strength of mine. Many consider that somewhat strange, in that I am generally thought of as a strong Type A personality – outgoing, more leader than follower. Despite that, I am less than comfortable when I have to go out and meet people for the first time. I'm not talking about working a trade show, but rather, when I find myself at events with my peers. Once the ice is broken, I do just great, but I have never really gotten into that initial "go out and meet them all and give them your company story," without the help of an introduction.

Of course, that doesn't mean networking – formally or informally – doesn't offer tremendous benefits to you or your company. The retreat I attended introduced me to several very interesting people and a couple of business opportunities, as well.

As I mentioned earlier, many of the people at that retreat were in the midst of change. One of them, shortly after the retreat, left a senior marketing position with a Fortune 100 company to join a modest-size investment banking firm. We happened to drive up to the retreat and back together. Sure enough, a couple of months later, I met with him and one of his partners, and less than four months after we met, the investment banking firm made us an offer to buy a stake in Presenting Solutions. That's pretty impressive networking.

Lesson #14: To some degree, networking is a numbers game. The more you are out there promoting your company to peers and other successful business people, the more likely you will find new opportunities.

Note that networking isn't just for the president of the company. It is a powerful tool that can be used by senior management, sales, and actually almost everyone in the company. And the good news is there's virtually no downside, except that it takes some of your time.

The Forest Through the Trees

It's time to revisit Lesson #1: Entrepreneurs just don't know when to quit, or rather, entrepreneurs often fail to recognize when they are out of their depth.

So I find myself at the beginning of 2001 with an investment banking firm looking to take a stake in the company and to take an active role in the company. For 15 years I've been telling people I understood that a company would need a leader with different skills and experience to take a company like ours to the next level.

And, bingo, here comes the offer! We have a couple of executive team meetings – shortly before and after the offer, to consider the value of accepting their offer. Everyone throws in an opinion, and even recognizing that the outside consultants have a vested interest in the status quo, we ultimately passed on the offer.

We had good reasons: The offer seemed low for the stake they wanted; they couldn't really explain to us exactly would happen, beyond their taking an active role and bringing scientific analysis of our business model. And then they would be drawing monies out for "consulting," which made the cash offer seem even lower. I really didn't have a good feel for how active they would be in the running of the company. I perceived it as ending up with another particularly expensive consulting team, not day-to-day, hands-on. They couldn't tell me specifically if, when, and how much money would be invested down the road, and so on.

I had lots of reservations, and we passed. Somehow, I forgot – or chose to forget – what I always considered a truth – Lesson #1!

What I didn't see (it's that 20-20 hindsight), is that they were offering the experience and the personnel to help us grow to the next level: Real process instead of shooting from the hip. I should have recognized that they were offering an opportunity for growth, based on building an intelligent business plan and good business practices. I certainly knew I wasn't the perfect company president, and I should have understood the potential evolution they could bring to Presenting Solutions.

The other point I missed at the time was that here was my fundable executive, actually wanting to invest in the company and join the management team. Unbelievable! As I said, I knew we needed one, but I didn't know how to go about finding one. And when one drops into our laps, I failed to recognize what I had been looking for.

I can comfortably say today that passing on their offer was as big a mistake as I have made in the 12 years of our company's existence. And it was all the worse a decision because I refused – or just failed – to see how they could benefit us, despite my real belief in Lesson #1. Bottom line: I found myself analyzing the components of their offer, instead of the big picture.

Lesson #15: Don't lose sight of the big picture. While the devil may be in the details, the details may be changed or renegotiated, but it's the sweeping impact of the big picture that you can't afford to lose sight of.

Building Character

So now its early 2001, and our industry is in a downturn. Our cost of advertising is through the roof, and our vendors are dumping product to our largest competitors in quantities we just can't handle and at prices that give them a tremendous edge and squeeze our margins.

Revenues drop. For the first time in company history, margins shrink. And to make matters worse, backend dollars for marketing start drying up. We're profitable in Q1, but some of that is annual backend dollars that come in from our largest suppliers – who are mostly on a March 31 fiscal year. Q2 comes around, and we're losing money. Q3 arrives, and we are hemorrhaging. And September 11 did real, additional damage to our sales.

I mentioned backend dollars. In our industry, they come in two flavors – marketing dollars and volume rebates. I'm still not sure that I made the right call. I needed to buy a lot to make my rebate numbers.

Consider this: Our largest vendor has an annual volume incentive rebate program, and our target was $6 million for their last fiscal year (ending 3-31-01). At $4.8 million, we get the minimum percentage – 0.5 percent, or $24,000; but at $6 million, we get the max – 3 percent – a whopping $180,000. Back then, and even now, that seems like way too much money to leave on the table. So, thanks to our vendor's flexibility, they let us buy $1 million worth of product the last week of March (on top of perhaps $300,000 of inventory already in-house). The result is that PS ends up sitting on a three-month supply in the first week of April. That promised to do serious damage to our cash flow, but considering the extra $156,000, it seemed well worth doing.

Our problem: While April and May revenues were soft (down about 8 percent from the previous year), the bottom fell out of the market in June, and we ended up 35 percent below the previous June – while inventory is at an all-time high. The two factors combined devastated cash flow and killed our ability to pay major vendors on a timely basis. From there, matters only got worse. Slow paying resulted in delays in getting product, which in turn cost us additional sales. Fortunately, our major vendors have come around and are keeping us in critical product, but for several months we lost 10 percent to 15 percent of potential sales because we couldn't deliver in a timely manner.

Lesson #16: Anticipate the best, but plan for the worst. Create contingency plans for unfavorable scenarios.

At no point did we look at the "what if" scenarios showing the outcome if sales were to drop 10 percent or 25 percent or 35 percent in one month, or, for that matter, a quarter or longer. So last June hurt us badly, and in late August, just when we were thinking our problems were fading, we were only two weeks from September 11, which set us back even further.

Reality check: By this time, late summer, I'm losing sleep, and despite significant cutbacks in payroll and advertising, the losses mount. We're not completely panicked, though; we start hiring to grow our sales force – moving more toward a sales driven model than our existing marketing driven model.

Now in the fairy tale, we hire a new sales manager. He or she hits the ground running and hires lots of sales people, and in no time our revenues are up, and profits are back.

No such luck! We found a sales manager, but we were unsuccessful in hitting our goals – from June to the end of September, we wanted to add a minimum of four (and ideally six) outside salespeople to our existing four. But October 1 came, and we had managed to hire only one. Too little, too late! While building up the sales force was a good idea (and we continue to do so), our problem was that we didn't have a well-designed plan to do so. Once again, it's that pesky ability to develop processes and execute them that we still hadn't mastered. Had we been better prepared, I believe we could have hit our targets

Return of the Fundable Executive

In September, that very same fundable executive gives me a call, just to touch base. As it turns out, I tell him about our reversal, and amazingly, after a few meetings and maybe 45 days, the investors again make an offer to take a stake in the company. Of course, the big bucks were gone, and the stake increased in size, but by then, we had managed to convert ourselves from a high-profile growth company to a shaky turnaround prospect.

When it comes down to the bottom line, I just didn't have a good handle on how to turn things around, and this professional and his company still saw big potential going forward. This time, I did what I should have done 10 months before – my wife and I signed on the dotted line.

Fewer than five days later, we had a new company president, and I'm bumped upstairs to CEO. In reality, though, I'm taking my cues from the president and learning volumes about process and execution. (They will never be my strong points, but at least I'm learning!)

Just barely 100 days later, while we're still losing money, it's truly amazing how much can get fixed in a short time. I'm deeply involved in many projects, but our president is the one driving the process and the execution, and it is working:

❑ Our relationships with key vendors have significantly improved, giving us the breathing room we need.
❑ We have overhauled our accounting department, correcting problems that occurred from trying to upgrade to MAS200 (a far more robust accounting software than we had), but doing the conversion without a good plan of implementation.
❑ We've decided to outsource our IT support. We have several servers in-house, but our Web sites are all hosted by top-tier Web hosting companies – after all, our Web sites are our primary sources of leads. Our expectation is reduced costs and higher reliability. We've interviewed several companies and will sign a contract soon.
❑ We've improved our gross profit margin by roughly two points in one month, thanks to identifying the problem, changing the commission structure, and asking the salespeople to make the effort.
❑ Our warranty and support programs, which are significant cash flow generators, were not performing well because of their high costs relative to the significantly lower selling prices of our products today, compared to a year or two ago. We identified the problem, dramatically reducing the selling prices, and in the first week of the new programs, we sold

our warranty program to 25 percent of new customers, up from 2 percent on the old program.

❑ We've managed to cancel most poorly performing advertising contracts and started a process that, for the first time, analyzes what's working and what's not.

❑ We have started recruiting more salespeople.

❑ We eliminated an initiative to sell Web-based conferencing. It's a good product, but it was sucking up badly needed resources and wouldn't be profitable for an absolute minimum of six to nine months. As things turn around, we will likely revisit it. Analysis, however, showed that now simply isn't the right time. Now is the time to focus on our core businesses.

❑ We reviewed our insurance policies and are modifying them to reduce our insurance costs by 10 to 15 percent.

❑ We've significantly improved morale!

❑ We gave our first merit raise in more than six months – on hold till now because of company finances.

❑ After concentrating on stabilizing operations and focusing on the day-to-day almost exclusively for 75 days, we recently started planning for the future again.

❑ There is a very visible light at the end of the tunnel!

There are lots of minor things happening as well, but what amazes me is that we were able to do even one quarter of this in 100 days. In the past that list would have taken a year or more to complete – except that probably a third of the initiatives would never have seen daylight. And that's the benefit of analyzing and planning over my shoot-from-the-hip-and-hope-it-works style.

Lesson #17: Identify needs; analyze options; make information-based decisions; plan the implementation; and execute.

Management Mining

Something new has happened at PS: Management is listening.

Actually, we're actively encouraging employees to take ownership and to help the company improve. Less than two weeks ago, we had our inside sales force, Webmaster, and customer service people in on a Saturday for a six-hour organized program designed to encourage everyone to contribute ideas, and even take turns facilitating the meeting. From that one meeting, points were made that resulted in the reworked warranty and support programs (that took two days) and some changes to our Web sites, and we identified ways to make our salespeople and customer service more efficient.

And that was just phase one. We will shortly bring in our outside sales force, along with others, for another "mining" session. And these sessions will continue as the company evolves.

"I'd Rather Be Lucky…"

Lesson #18: Given a choice between Lucky and Good, be BOTH! In fact, I think of it this way: Lucky is the great ideas; Good is the ability to take those ideas and execute – "run with it."

If PS can do both, we should be back on the fast-growth track in no time.

So Much to Learn

There's much left to do, and I'm sure much more to learn as Presenting Solutions goes forward – and it's awfully nice to be going forward again. We are expecting profitability to return in the next quarter, along with new credit lines and a capital infusion, and new projects and new growth in the second half of the year.

Here are a few last thoughts that are straightforward enough that they don't need a story to illustrate them.

Lesson #19: Get the most out of your employees. Motivate them; get them to take ownership in the success of the company. Team meetings and "management mining" are two tools you can use.

Lesson #20: Don't lose sight of your core business. Build on it; find growth in areas that complement it.

Lesson #21: Review your business model on a regular basis. Is it working? Will it carry you forward, or do you need to change it?

One last piece of advice: Pay attention! Great opportunities (and potential pitfalls) are all around. Avoid tunnel vision, and don't get so caught up in your own belief set that you don't recognize the opportunities or heed the warnings. Keep one eye on the big picture at all times; surround your self with good, experienced people; and have some fun!

Art Feierman is a third-generation entrepreneur and sales professional. He is also considered something of pioneer of the World Wide Web, launching his first major site in early 1995. He is the CEO and founder of Presenting Solutions, LLC, a 12-year-old company dedicated to empowering effective communications. His Web-centric company offers valued-added solutions built around presentation equipment and audio-visual integration and includes portable LCD projectors and plasma displays. Presenting Solutions operates multiple Web sites, including presentingsolutions.com, its primary, content-rich Web site, and powerpointers.com, a knowledgebase of articles by professional speakers, covering a wide range of communications and presentation skills. He publishes the 2thePoint newsletter and The Quarterly Portable Projector Report.

Mr. Feierman has been an occasional public speaker for the past 20 years, primarily engaging audiences on both effective communications and presentation technologies. He has spoken at a wide range of events, including computer shows, medical conferences, and events sponsored by such companies as Apple Computer and Epson America

Before his 16 years in the presentations industry, Mr. Feierman held several positions with Epson America, first building and conducting a dealer sales training program for hundreds of dealer salespeople, and later, as a top-producing major accounts sales manager.

After graduating from Penn State University 1972, Mr. Feierman spent a decade in the consumer electronics and early PC industries.

The Format of Aspatore Entrepreneurial Review

Aspatore Entrepreneurial Review is an interactive journal based on the submission of white papers, articles and knowledge excerpts from partner level venture capitalists and C-Level (CEO, CTO, CFO, CMO) executives from the world's top firms and companies.

Each Aspatore Entrepreneurial Review follows the following special format, specifically designed by venture capitalists and entrepreneurs as the preferred way to comprehend business intelligence:

I. Executive Summary
The Executive Summary provides the highlight of the current journal, and enables you to very quickly scan the most important concepts.

II. AER Feature
The AER Feature focuses on a specific topic currently affecting venture professionals and entrepreneurs.

III. In The Know
In the Know features knowledge excerpts from leading venture professionals and entrepreneurs on a variety of topics, enabling you to expand your breadth of knowledge, communicate intelligently on a wide range of important issues, and develop ideas for innovation and new revenue opportunities within your own area of expertise.

IV. Executive Perspectives
Executive Perspectives feature white papers on a variety of topics affecting venture professionals and entrepreneurs, submitted by partners from leading venture firms.

V. Profession Spotlight
The Profession Spotlight focuses on a key C-Level (CEO, CFO, CTO, CFO, CMO, COO, Partner) or executive position, and the "Golden Rules" of that profession and other topics that will enable other types of executives to identify efficiencies, new product/service ideas, new revenue opportunities, interact better and implement innovative concepts into their own profession.

VI. Industry Spotlight
The Industry Spotlight section highlights current industries (such as wireless, technology, health care, services and more), or part of an industry, that is affecting the majority of businesses in some way or another and provides opportunities for growth and new profit centers.

VII. Ideas For Innovation
Ideas for Innovation features a series of question blocks that can be used as a starting point for an executive meeting, brainstorming session, or distributed to key partners or management team executives as a way to stimulate new ideas.

To Order, Visit Us At www.Aspatore.com Or Call Toll Free 1-866-Aspatore (277-2867)

ASPATORE ENTREPRENEURIAL REVIEW-ORDER FORM

Call Us Toll Free at 1-866-Aspatore (277-2867)
Or Tear Out This Page and Mail or Fax To:
Aspatore Books, PO Box 883, Bedford, MA 01730
Or Fax To (617) 249-1970 (Preferred)

Name:

E-mail:

Shipping Address:

City: State: Zip:

Billing Address:

City: State: Zip:

Phone:

Please Circle the Journal (s) You Would like to Subscribe to:
Aspatore Business Review   Aspatore Entrepreneurial Review
Aspatore Marketing Review   Aspatore Technology Review
Aspatore Law Review   Aspatore Investing Review

Lock in at the Current Rates Today-Rates Increase Every Year
Please Check the Desired Length Subscription:
1 Year ($1,090) _____   2 Years (Save 10%-$1,962) _____
5 Years (Save 20%-$4,360) _____   10 Years (Save 30%-$7,630) _____
Lifetime Subscription ($24,980) _____

Number of Subscriptions _____ (3-4 subscriptions-10% discount, 5-10 subscriptions-15% discount, 11-20 subscriptions-20% discount, 21-50 subscriptions-30% discount, 51+ subscriptions-40% discount) If multiple year subscription is ordered, discount will be added to previous discount. If nothing is entered, we shall process the order for 1 subscription.

(If mailing in a check you can skip this section but please read fine print below and sign below)
Credit Card Type (Visa & Mastercard & Amex):

Credit Card Number:

Expiration Date:

Signature:

Would you like us to automatically bill your credit card at the end of your subscription so there is no discontinuity in service? (You can still cancel your subscription at any point before the renewal date.) Please circle: Yes   No

*(Please note the billing address much match the address on file with your credit card company exactly)

Terms & Conditions-We shall send a confirmation receipt to your e-mail address. If ordering from Massachusetts, please add 5% sales tax on the order (not including shipping and handling). If ordering from outside of the US, an additional $51.95 per year will be charged for shipping and handling costs. All issues are paperback and will be shipped as soon as they become available. Sorry, no returns, cancellations or refunds at any point unless automatic billing is selected, at which point you may cancel at any time before your subscription is renewed (no funds shall be returned however for the period currently subscribed to). Issues that are not already published will be shipped upon publication date. Publication dates are subject to delay-please allow 1-2 weeks for delivery of first issue. If a new issue is not coming out for another month, the issue from the previous quarter will be sent for the first issue.

To Order, Visit Us At www.Aspatore.com Or
Call Toll Free 1-866-Aspatore (277-2867)

BUILD YOUR OWN BUSINESS LIBRARY

Option A: Receive Every Book Published by Aspatore Books-Only $1,089 a Year-
A Savings of Over 60% Off Retail prices

Receive every book published by Aspatore Books every year-between 60-100 books-a must have on bookshelves of every executive and an invaluable resource for quick access, business intelligence from industry insiders. Or send the collection as a gift to someone else!

The Aspatore Business Library Collection features must have business books on various positions, industries and topics, creating the ultimate business library for business professionals. The books in the collection feature business intelligence from C-Level executives (CEO, CTO, CFO, CMO, CFO, Partner) from the world's most respected companies, and represent an invaluable resource for quick access, business intelligence from industry insiders on a wide range of topics. Every business professional should have their own executive library, such as the top executives and great business leaders of our time have always had. The Aspatore Business Library Collection features the most exclusive, biggest name executives of our time and their most insightful words of wisdom, creating the ultimate executive library. Upon order being placed, you will immediately receive books published within the last month, and then for 11 months going forward (you also receive all titles 1-3 months before retail stores receive the new book). You may even request up to 10 books already published by Aspatore Books to be included.

Option B: 25 Best Selling Business Books-Only $399-A Savings of Over 45%Off Retail Prices!

Buy the top 25 best selling business titles published by Aspatore Books, a must have on bookshelves of every executive and an invaluable resource for quick access, business intelligence from industry insiders. Or send the collection as a gift to someone else! These books feature business intelligence from C-Level executives (CEO, CTO, CFO, CMO, CFO, Partner) from over half the world's 500 largest companies. Although every book may not be in your exact area of specialty, having these books on hand will time and again serve as incredible resources for you and everyone in your office. These books provide a wide array of information on various positions, industries and topics, creating a complete business library unto themselves. If you already have one or more of these books, please note this on the order form and different books will be added.

To Order, Visit Us At www.Aspatore.com Or Call Toll Free 1-866-Aspatore (277-2867)

Books Included:

Inside the Minds: The Wireless Industry-Industry Leaders Share Their Knowledge on the Future of the Wireless Revolution

Inside the Minds: Leading Consultants-Industry Leaders Share Their Knowledge on the Future of the Consulting Profession and Industry

Inside the Minds: Leading Deal Makers-Industry Leaders Share Their Knowledge on Negotiations, Leveraging Your Position and the Art of Deal Making

Inside the Minds: The Semiconductor Industry-Industry Leaders Share Their Knowledge on the Future of the Semiconductor Revolution

Inside the Minds: Leading Advertisers-Industry Leaders Share Their Knowledge on the Future of Advertising, Marketing and Building Successful Brands

Inside the Minds: Leading Accountants-Industry Leaders Share Their Knowledge on the Future of the Accounting Industry & Profession

Inside the Minds: The New Health Care Industry-Industry Leaders Share Their Knowledge on the Future of the Technology Charged Health Care Industry

Inside the Minds: Leading IP Lawyers-Leading IP Lawyers Share Their Knowledge on the Art & Science of Intellectual Property

Inside the Minds: Leading Labor Lawyers-Leading Labor Lawyers Share Their Knowledge on the Art & Science of Labor Law

Inside the Minds: Leading Litigators-Leading Litigators Share Their Knowledge on the Art & Science of Litigation

Inside the Minds: The Art of Public Relations-PR Visionaries Reveal the Secrets to Getting Noticed, Making a Name for Your Company, and Building a Brand Through Public Relations

Inside the Minds: Venture Capitalists-Inside the High Stakes and Fast Moving World of Venture Capital

Bigwig Briefs: Term Sheets & Valuations-An Inside Look at the Intricacies of Term Sheets & Valuations

Bigwig Briefs: Hunting Venture Capital-An Inside Look at the Basics of Venture Capital

Inside the Minds: Leading Wall St. Investors-Financial Gurus Reveal the Secrets to Picking a Winning Portfolio

Inside the Minds: Leading Marketers-Industry Leaders Share Their Knowledge on Building Successful Brands

Inside the Minds: Chief Technology Officers-Industry Experts Reveal the Secrets to Developing, Implementing, and Capitalizing on the Best Technologies in the World

Inside the Minds: Internet Bizdev-Industry Experts Reveal the Secrets to Inking Deals in the Internet Industry

Inside the Minds: The Entrepreneurial Problem Solver-Getting Yourself & Others to Think More Like an Entrepreneur

Inside the Minds: Internet Bigwigs-Internet CEOs and Research Analysts Forecast the Future of the Internet Economy

Inside the Minds: Leading CEOs-The Secrets to Management, Leadership & Profiting in Any Economy

Inside the Minds: Internet Marketing-Industry Experts Reveal the Secrets to Marketing, Advertising, and Building a Successful Brand on the Internet

Inside the Minds: Leading CTOs-Industry Leaders Share Their Knowledge on Harnessing and Developing the Best Technologies

Bigwig Briefs: Guerrilla Marketing-The Best of Guerrilla Marketing

Oh Behave! Reinforcing Successful Behaviors at Work With Consequences

BUILD YOUR OWN BUSINESS LIBRARY

Call Us Toll Free at 1-866-Aspatore (277-2867)
Or Tear Out This Page and Mail or Fax To:
Aspatore Books, PO Box 883, Bedford, MA 01730
Or Fax To (617) 249-1970 (Preferred)

Name:

E-mail:

Shipping Address:

City: State: Zip:

Billing Address:

City: State: Zip:

Phone:

Please Check Option A or Option B:

Option A _____ (Receive Every Book Published by Aspatore Books-$1,089 a Year)
Please indicate here any titles already published by Aspatore Books you would like in addition (there will be no charge for these titles as they will be included as part of the first month of books):

_____

_____

_____

_____

Option B _____ (25 Best Selling Business Books-$399)
Please indicate here any titles you already currently have (other best selling titles on a similar topic will then be added in their place):

_____

_____

_____

(If mailing in a check you can skip this section but please read fine print below and sign below)
Credit Card Type (Visa & Mastercard & Amex):

Credit Card Number:

Expiration Date:

Signature:

If option A is chosen, would you like us to automatically bill your credit card at the end of your subscription so there is no discontinuity in service? (You can still cancel your subscription at any point before the renewal date.) Please check: Yes _____   No _____

*(Please note the billing address much match the address on file with your credit card company exactly)

Terms & Conditions-We shall send a confirmation receipt to your e-mail address. If ordering from Massachusetts, please add 5% sales tax on the order (not including shipping and handling). If ordering from outside of the US, an additional $300 in shipping and handling costs will be charged for Option A and an additional $125 for Option B. All books are paperback and will be shipped as soon as they become available. Total number of books for Option A will vary from year to year, between 60-100 books. Sorry, no returns or refunds at any point unless automatic billing is selected, at which point you may cancel at any time before your subscription is renewed (no funds shall be returned however for the period currently subscribed to). Books that are not already published will be shipped upon publication date. Publication dates are subject to delay-please allow 1-2 weeks for delivery of first books. For the most up to date information on publication dates and availability please visit www.Aspatore.com.

To Order, Visit Us At www.Aspatore.com Or
Call Toll Free 1-866-Aspatore (277-2867)

THE FOCUSBOOK™
ASSEMBLE YOUR OWN
BUSINESS BOOK™

Ever wish you could assemble your own business book, and even add your own thoughts in the book? Here is your chance to become the managing editor or your own book!

The Focusbook™ enables you to become the managing editor of your own book, by selecting individual chapters from the best selling business books published by Aspatore Books to assemble your own business book. A Focusbook™ can highlight a particular topic, industry, or area of expertise for yourself, your team, your course, or even your entire company. You can even add additional text of your own to the book, such as reference information, points to focus on, or even a course syllabus, in order to further customize it to better suit your needs. The Focusbook™ is the future of business books, allowing you to become the managing editor of your own business book, based on what you deem important, enabling yourself, and others to focus, innovate and outperform.

How It Works:
1. Select up to 10, 15, or 25 chapters from the choices on the following pages by checking the appropriate boxes. (Each Chapter Ranges From 15-40 Pages)
2. Decide if you want to include any of your own text to the book—maybe an introduction (as to why you chose these chapters), employee instructions (for new hires or to use as a management course/refresher), a course syllabus, information so it is applicable for clients/customers (reference), or even an article/white paper you already wrote. (Please note Aspatore Books will not edit the work, it is simply printed as is. Aspatore Books will not be considered the publisher of any additions and you will retain all rights to that content.)
3. Decide on a quantity.

**To Order, Visit Us At www.Aspatore.com Or
Call Toll Free 1-866-Aspatore (277-2867)**

How the Book Will Look:

1. The book will be 5 inches tall and 8 inches wide (on the front and back). The width will vary depending on the amount of text. The book will look like a normal business book found in bookstores nationwide.

2. On the cover of the book, it will read "A Focusbook™ Assembled By," with your name on the next line (Jason Phillips in the example above). We can also add a company/university/course name if you so choose. Your name will also appear on the spine of the book. You can then also select a title for your Focusbook™ (such as Marketing Smarts as depicted in the picture above). On the back of the book will be the chapter names from your book.

3. The book will feature the standard Focusbook™ cover (see above), with the dominant colors being black with a red stripe across.

4. The chapters will be placed in a random order, unless a specific order is instructed on the order form. If you are adding your own text, it can be placed at the beginning or the end of the text.

5. The book will feature the chapters you selected, plus any content of your own (optional), and a special section at the end for notes and ideas of your own to add as you read through and refer back to your Focusbook™.

Select the Chapters You Want on the Following Pages Then Fill Out the Order Form at the End

To Order, Visit Us At www.Aspatore.com Or Call Toll Free 1-866-Aspatore (277-2867)

Chapter #/Title	Author	Units
VENTURE CAPITAL/ENTREPRENEURSHIP		
123. *Developing the Right Team Strategy	Sam Colella (Versant Ventures, Managing Director)	1
124. *Successful Deal Doing	Patrick Ennis (ARCH Venture Partners, Partner)	1
125. *Deal Making: The Interpersonal Aspects	John M. Abraham (Battery Ventures, Venture Partner)	1
126. *The Art of Negotiations	Robert Chefitz (APAX Partners, General Partner)	1
127. Future Opportunities	Michael Moritz (Sequoia Capital)	1
128. *What VCs Look For	Heidi Roizen (SOFTBANK Venture Capital)	1
129. International Opportunities	Jan Henric Buettner (Bertelsmann Ventures)	1
130. The Importance of Technology	Alex Wilmerding (Boston Capital Ventures)	1
131. Next Generation Success	Andrew Filipowski (divine interVentures)	1
132. Internet Business Models	Suzanne King (New Enterprise Associates)	1
133. Valuations and Key Indicators	Jonathan Goldstein (TA Associates)	1
134. Early Stage Investing	Virginia Bonker (Blue Rock Capital)	1
135. Calculating Risk	Guy Bradley (CMGI @ Ventures)	1
136. *Focus on Technology	Stephan Andriole (Safeguard Scientifics, Inc.)	1
137. Evaluating Business Models	Marc Benson (Mid-Atlantic Venture Funds)	1
138. Early Stage Valuations and Keys to Success	Roger Novak, Jack Biddle (Novak Biddle Venture Partners)	1
139. The Importance of People and the Market	Nuri Wissa (Kestrel Venture Management)	1
140. Focused Investing	Mark Lotke (Internet Capital Group)	1

* Denotes Best Selling Chapter

Chapter #/Title	Author	Units
141. *Term Sheet Basics	Alex Wilmerding (Boston Capital Ventures)	1
142. *How to Examine a Term Sheet	Alex Wilmerding (Boston Capital Ventures)	1
143. * A Section-by-Section View of a Term Sheet	Alex Wilmerding (Boston Capital Ventures)	4
144. *Valuations and the Term Sheet	Alex Wilmerding (Boston Capital Ventures)	1
145. Marketing Your Business to Investors	Harrison Smith (Krooth & Altman, Partner)	1
146. Essential Elements in Executive Summaries	Harrison Smith (Krooth & Altman, Partner)	1
267. *The Journey to Entrepreneurship	Dave Cone (Camstar, CEO)	1
268. *Founding a Business on Principles	Steve Demos (White Wave, Founder & President)	1
269. *Entrepreneur 101-From Validation to Viability	Mike Turner (Waveset Technologies, CEO)	1
270. Entrepreneurship Through Choppy Waters	Frederick Beer (Auragen Communications, CEO)	1
271. The World of Entrepreneurial Momentum	Hatch Graham (Bandwidth9, CEO)	1
271. The Extreme Entrepreneur	Todd Parent (Extreme Pizza, CEO)	1
272. * An Entrepreneur's Blueprint for Success	Farsheed Ferdowsi (Paymaxx, CEO)	1
273. From Mom & Pop to National Player	Jack Lavin (Arrow Financial Services, CEO)	1
274. Better to Be a PT Boat Than a Battleship	Lucinda Duncalfe Holt (Destiny, CEO)	1
275. *Lessons Learned for Entrepreneurs	Art Feierman (Presenting Solutions. CEO)	1

MARKETING/ADVERTISING/PR

Chapter #/Title	Author	Units
1. *Connecting With Consumer Needs	Stephen Jones (Coca-Cola, Chief Marketing Officer)	1
2. Staying Customer Focused	T. Michael Glenn (FedEx, EVP Market Development)	1
3. Building an Internet Mega-Brand	Karen Edwards (Yahoo!, VP, Brand Marketing)	1

* Denotes Best Selling Chapter

Chapter #/Title	Author	Units
4. Giving the Consumer a Seat at the Table	Michael Linton (Best Buy, SVP Marketing)	1
5. Building a Powerful Marketing Engine	Jody Bilney (Verizon, SVP Brand Management)	1
6. *Brands and Marketing: Evolving Together	John Hayes (American Express, EVP Brand Management)	1
7. Marlboro Friday: Branding a Product	Richard Rivers (Unilever, SVP)	1
8. Marketing Success: Providing Choice	Richard Costello (GE, Corporate Marketing Manager)	1
9. Turning a Brand Into a National Pastime	Tim Brosnan (Major League Baseball, EVP Business)	1
10. Advertisers' Conundrum-Change or Be Changed	M T Rainey (Young & Rubicam, Co-CEO)	1
11. *Rallying the Troops in Advertising	Eric Rosenkranz (Grey, CEO Asia Pacific)	1
12. Achieving Success as an Advertising Team	David Bell (Interpublic Group, Vice Chairman)	1
13. *Advertising: Invitation Only, No Regrets	Bob Brennan (Leo Burnett Worldwide, President)	1
14. *The Secret to Global Lovemark Brands	Tim Love (Saatchi & Saatchi, Managing Partner)	1
15. Soak it All In-The Secrets to Advertising Success	Paul Simons (Ogilvy Mather UK, CEO)	1
16. Likeable Advertising: Creative That Works	Alan Kalter (Doner, CEO)	1
17. Advertising Success: Tuning Into the Consumer	Alan Schultz (Valassis, CEO)	1
18. The Client Perspective in Advertising	Brendan Ryan (FCB Worldwide, CEO)	1
19. *Advertising Results in the Age of the Internet	David Kenny (Digitas, CEO)	1
20. *Communications for Tomorrow's Leaders	Christopher Komisarjevsky (Burson-Marsteller, CEO)	2
21. The Creation of Trust	Rich Jernstedt (Golin/Harris International, CEO)	1
22. *Prosumer: A New Breed of Proactive Consumer	Don Middleberg (Middleberg Euro RSCG, CEO)	1
23. *The Power of PR in a Complex World	Richard Edelman (Edelman PR, CEO)	1
24. Success in Public Relations	Lou Rena Hammond (Lou Hammond & Assoc., President)	1

* Denotes Best Selling Chapter

Chapter #/Title	Author	Units
25. The Art and Science of Public Relations	Anthony Russo, Ph.D. (Noonan Russo Communications, CEO)	1
26. Critical Elements of Success in PR	Thomas Amberg (Cushman Amberg Communications, CEO)	1
27. Small Business PR Bang!	Robyn M. Sachs (RMR & Associates, CEO)	1
28. PR: A Key Driver of Brand Marketing	Patrice Tanaka (Patrice Tanaka & Company, Inc., CEO)	1
29. PR: Essential Function in a Democratic Society	David Finn (Ruder Finn Group, Chairman)	1
30. *21st Century Public Relations	Larry Weber (Weber Shandwick Worldwide, Founder)	1
31. *Public Relations as an Art and a Craft	Ron Watt (Watt/Fleishman-Hillard Inc., CEO)	1
32. Connecting the Client With Their Public	David Copithorne (Porter Novelli International, CEO)	1
33. PR: Becoming the Preferred Strategic Tool	Aedhmar Hynes (Text 100, CEO)	1
34. Public Relations Today and Tomorrow	Herbert L. Corbin (KCSA PR, Managing Partner)	1
35. Delivering a High Quality, Measurable Service	David Paine (PainePR, President)	1
36. *The Impact of High-Technology PR	Steve Schwartz (Schwartz Comm., President)	1
37. The Emotional Quotient of the Target Audience	Lee Duffey (Duffey Communications, President)	1
38. The Service Element in Successful PR	Andrea Carney (Brodeur Worldwide, CEO)	1
39. Helping Clients Achieve Their True PE Ratio	Scott Chaikin (Dix & Eaton, Chairman and CEO)	1
40. The Art of Public Relations	Dan Klores (Dan Klores Communications, President)	1
41. Passion and Precision in Communication	Raymond L. Kotcher (Ketchum, CEO)	1
42. Professionalism and Success in Public Relations	Victor Kamber (The Kamber Group, CEO)	1
43. A Balanced Internet Marketing Program	Meg Brossy (24/7 Media, Chief Marketing Officer)	1
44. *Internet Guerrilla Marketing on a Budget	Jay Levinson (Best-Selling Author)	1
45. Narrowcasting Through Email Marketing	Joe Payne (Microstrategy, Chief Marketing Officer)	1

* Denotes Best Selling Chapter

Chapter #/Title	Author	Units
46. Targeted Internet Marketing Strategies	John Ferber (Advertising.com, Founder)	1
47. Incentive Marketing on the Internet	Steve Parker (MyPoints, SVP Marketing)	1
48. B2B Internet Marketing	Tara Knowles (Viant, Chief Marketing Officer)	1
49. Breaking Through the Clutter on the Internet	Wenda Harris (Doubleclick, EVP General Network)	1
50. Measuring ROI Across Different Mediums	Mark Delvecchio (eWanted.com, VP Marketing)	1
51. *What is Guerrilla Marketing?	Jay Levinson (Best-Selling Author)	1
52. *What Makes a Guerrilla?	Jay Levinson (Best-Selling Author)	1
53. *Guerrilla Marketing: Attacking the Market	Jay Levinson (Best-Selling Author)	1
86. *Everyone is a Marketer	Jay Levinson (Best-Selling Author)	1
87. *Media Choices for the Guerrilla Marketer	Jay Levinson (Best-Selling Author)	1
88. *Technology and the Guerrilla Marketer	Jay Levinson (Best-Selling Author)	1
107. *Guerrilla Marketing on a Budget	Jay Levinson (Best-Selling Author)	1

MANAGEMENT/ CONSULTING

Chapter #/Title	Author	Units
276. *Maintaining Values in a Culture of Change	Richard Priory (Duke Energy, CEO)	1
69. *Fundamentals Never Go Out of Style	Fred Poses (American Standard, CEO)	1
70. High-Tech Company, High-Touch Values	John W. Loose (Corning, CEO)	1
71. Balancing Priorities for the Bottom Line	Bruce Nelson (Office Depot, Chairman)	1
72. *Keeping the Right People With Your Company	Thomas C. Sullivan (RPM, CEO)	1
73. *Gaining Entrepreneurial Momentum	Myron P. Shevell (New England Motor Freight, CEO)	1

* Denotes Best Selling Chapter

Chapter #/Title	Author	Units
74. Creating a Culture That Ensures Success	Justin Jaschke (Verio, CEO)	1
54. *The Drive for Business Results	Frank Roney (IBM, General Manager)	1
55. *Understanding the Client	Randolph C. Blazer (KPMG Consulting, Inc., CEO)	1
56. *The Interface of Technology and Business	Pamela McNamara (Arthur D. Little, Inc., CEO)	1
57. *Elements of the Strategy Consulting Business	Dr. Chuck Lucier (Booz-Allan & Hamilton, SVP)	1
58. *Consulting: Figuring Out How to Do it Right	Dietmarr Osterman (A.T. Kearney, CEO)	1
195. Client Value in Consulting	Luther J. Nussbaum (First Consulting Group, CEO)	1
196. The Rules Have Changed in Consulting	John C. McAuliffe (General Physics Corporation, President)	1
197. Tailoring Solutions to Meet Client Needs	Thomas J. Silveri (Drake Beam Morin, CEO)	1
198. *The Future of Marketing Consulting	Davis Frigstad (Frost & Sullivan, Chairman)	1
59. *Setting and Achieving Goals (For Women)	Jennifer Openshaw (Women's Financial Network)	1
60. The Path to Success (For Women)	Tiffany Bass Bukow (MsMoney, Founder and CEO)	2
61. Becoming a Leader (For Women)	Patricia Dunn (Barclays Global Investors, CEO)	1
62. Career Transitions (For Women)	Vivian Banta (Prudential Financial, CEO)	1
63. Making the Most of Your Time (For Women)	Kerri Lee Sinclair (AgentArts, Managing Director)	1
64. Follow Your Dreams (For Women)	Kim Fischer (AudioBasket, Co-Founder and CEO)	1
65. Keep Learning (For Women)	Krishna Subramanian (Kovair, CEO)	1
66. Keep Perspective (For Women)	Mona Lisa Wallace (RealEco.com, CEO)	1
67. Experiment With Different Things (For Women)	Emily Hofstetter (SiliconSalley.com, CEO)	1
68. Do What You Enjoy (For Women)	Lisa Henderson (LevelEdge, Founder and CEO)	1

* Denotes Best Selling Chapter

Chapter #	Title	Author	Units
	LAW		
75.	*Navigating Labor Law	Charles Birenbaum (Thelan Reid & Priest, Labor Chair)	1
76.	The Makings of a Great Labor Lawyer	Gary Klotz (Butzel Long, Labor Chair)	1
77.	The Complexity of Labor Law	Michael Reynvaan (Perkins Coie, Labor Chair)	1
78.	*Labor Lawyer Code: Integrity and Honesty	Max Brittain, Jr. (Schiff Hardin & Waite, Labor Chair)	1
89.	The Litigator: Advocate and Counselor	Rob Johnson (Sonnenschein Nath, Litigation Chair)	1
90.	*The Key to Success in Litigation: Empathy	John Strauch (Jones, Day, Reavis & Pogue, Litigation Chair)	1
91.	*Major Corporate and Commercial Litigation	Jeffrey Barist (Milbank, Tweed, Hadley, Litigation Chair)	1
92.	Keys to Success as a Litigator	Martin Flumenbaum (Paul, Weiss, Rifkind, Litigation Chair)	1
93.	*Deciding When to Go to Trial	Martin Lueck (Robins, Kaplan, Miller, Litigation Chair)	1
94.	Credibility and Persuasiveness in Litigation	Michael Feldberg (Schulte Roth & Zabel, Litigation Chair)	1
95.	*Litigation Challenges in the 21st Century	Thomas Kilbane (Squire, Sanders, Dempsey, Litigation Chair)	1
96.	*Keeping it Simple	Evan R. Chesler (Cravath, Swaine & Moore, Litigation Chair)	1
97.	Assessing Risk Through Preparation & Honesty	Harvey Kurzweil (Dewey Ballantine, Litigation Chair)	1
98.	The Essence of Success: Solving the Problem	James W. Quinn (Weil, Gotshal & Manges, Litigation Chair)	1
99.	The Performance Aspect of Litigation	Charles E. Koob (Simpson Thacher Bartlett, Litigation Chair)	1
100.	*The Future of IP: Intellectual Asset Mngmnt.	Richard S. Florsheim (Foley & Lardner, IP Chair)	1
101.	The Balancing of Art & Science in IP Law	Victor M. Wigman (Blank Rome, IP Chair)	1
102.	*Policing a Trademark	Paula J. Krasny (Baker & McKenzie, IP Chair)	1
103.	Credibility & Candor: Must Have Skills	Brandon Baum (Cooley Godward, IP Litigation Chair)	1
104.	The Art & Science of Patent Law	Stuart Lubitz (Hogan & Hartson, Partner)	1

* **Denotes Best Selling Chapter**

Chapter #/Title	Author	Units
105. Successful IP Litigation	Cecilia Gonzalez (Howrey Simon Arnold & White, IP Chair)	1
106. Achieving Recognized Value in Ideas	Dean Russell (Kilpatrick Stockton, IP Chair)	1
108. Keeping Current W/ Rapidly Changing Times	Bruce Keller (Debevoise & Plimpton, IP Litigation Chair)	1
109. *Maximizing the Value of an IP Portfolio	Roger Maxwell (Jenkins & Gilchrist, IP Chair)	2
110. *The Power of Experience in Deal Making	Joseph Hoffman (Arter & Hadden, Corporate/Securities Chair)	1
111. *The Deal: The Beginning Rather than the End	Mark Macenka (Testa, Hurwitz & Thibeault, Business Chair)	1
112. Communicating With Clients	Gerard S. DiFiore (Reed Smith, Corporate/Securities Chair)	1
113. Making a Deal Work	Kenneth S. Bezozo, (Haynes and Boone, Business Chair)	1
114. Challenges for Internet & Tech. Companies	Carl Cohen (Buchanan Ingersoll, Technology Chair)	1
115. The Copyright Revolution	Mark Fischer (Palmer & Dodge, Internet/E-Commerce Chair)	1
116. Privacy Rights and Ownership of Content	Brian Vandenberg (uBid.com, General Counsel)	1
117. Business Intelligence From Day One	Mark I. Gruhin (Schmeltzer, Aptaker and Shepard, , Partner)	1
118. Legal Rules for Internet Companies	Arnold Levine (Proskauer Rose LLP, Chair, iPractice Group)	1
119. Protecting Your Assets	Gordon Caplan (Mintz Levin PC)	1
120. The Golden Rules of Raising Capital	James Hutchinson (Hogan & Hartson LLP)	1
121. Identifying the Right Legal Challenges	John Igeo (Encore Development, General Counsel)	1
122. The Importance of Patents	Richard Turner (Sughrue, Mion,, Senior Counsel)	1
79. *Common Values in Employment Law	Columbus Gangemi, Jr. (Winston & Strawn, Labor Chair)	1
80. Building Long Term Relationships with Clients	Fred Alvarez (Wilson Sonsini, Labor Chair)	1
81. *Becoming Part of the Client's Success	Brian Gold (Sidley Austin Brown & Wood, Labor Chair)	1
82. *Understanding Multiple Audiences	Raymond Wheeler (Morrison & Foerster, Labor Chair)	1

* Denotes Best Selling Chapter

Chapter #/Title	Author	Units
83. Employment Lawyer: Advisor and Advocate	Judith Langevin (Gray, Plant, Mooty & Bennett, Labor Chair)	1
84. *Bringing Added Value to the Deal Practice	Mary Ann Jorgenson (Squires Sanders Dempsey, Labor Chair)	1
85. Traditional Legal Matters on the Internet	Harrison Smith (Krooth & Altman LLP, Partner)	1

TECHNOLOGY/INTERNET

Chapter #/Title	Author	Units
167. *Closing the Technology Gap	Dr. Carl S. Ledbetter (Novell, CTO)	1
168. *Creating and Enriching Business Value	Richard Schroth (Perot Systems, CTO)	1
169. *Innovation Drives Business Success	Kirill Tatarinov (BMC Software, Senior Vice President, CTO)	1
170. *Managing the Technology Knowledge	Dr. Scott Dietzen (BEA E-Commerce Server Division, CTO)	1
171. The CTO as an Agent of Change	Doug Cavit (McAfee.com, CTO)	1
172. The Class Struggle and The CTO	Dan Woods (Capital Thinking, CTO)	1
173. A CTO's Perspective on the Role of a CTO	Mike Toma (eLabor, CTO)	1
174. Technology Solutions to Business Needs	Michael S. Dunn (Encoda Systems, CTO, EVP)	1
175. Bridging Business and Technology	Mike Ragunas (StaplesDirect.com, CTO)	1
176. *The Art of Being a CTO - Fostering Change	Rick Bergquist (PeopleSoft, CTO)	1
178. Developing Best of Breed Technologies	Dr. David Whelan (Boeing, Space and Communications, CTO)	1
179. *Technology as a Strategic Weapon	Kevin Vasconi (Covisint, CTO)	1
180. Role of the CTO in a Venture-Backed Startup	Dan Burgin (Finali, CTO)	1
181. *Leading Technology During Turbulent Times	Frank Campagnoni (GE Global eXchange Services, CTO)	1
182. Staying on Top of Changing Technologies	Andrew Wolfe (SONICblue (formerly S3), CTO)	1

* Denotes Best Selling Chapter

Chapter #/Title	Author	Units
183. Building What the Market Needs	Neil Webber (Vignette, Former CTO, Co-Founder)	1
184. *Let the Business Dictate the Technology	Dwight Gibbs (The Motley Fool, Chief Techie Geek)	1
185. Technology Solutions: From the Ground Up	Peter Stern (Datek, CTO)	1
186. The Securities Behind Technology	Warwick Ford (VeriSign, CTO)	1
187. Building Leading Technology	Ron Moritz (Symantec, CTO)	1
188. The Business Sense Behind Technology	Dermot McCormack (Flooz.com, CTO and Co-Founder)	1
189. A Simple and Scaleable Technology Interface	Pavan Nigam (WebMD, Former CTO/Co-Fndr, Healtheon)	1
190. Designing the Right Technology Solution	Michael Wolfe (Kana Communications, VP, Engineering)	1
191. The Role of a CTO	Daniel Jaye (Engage, CTO and Co-Founder)	1
147. *Wireless Technology: Make It Simple	John Zeglis (AT&T Wireless, CEO)	1
148. *Bringing Value to the Consumer	Patrick McVeigh (OmniSky, Chairman and CEO)	1
149. Wireless Challenges	Sanjoy Malik (Air2Web, Founder, President and CEO)	1
150. The High Costs of Wireless	Paul Sethy (AirPrime, Founder & Chairman)	1
151. Developing Areas of Wireless	Reza Ahy (Aperto Networks, President & CEO)	1
152. *The Real Potential for Wireless	Martin Cooper (Arraycomm, Chairman & CEO)	1
153. Bringing Wireless into the Mainstream	Robert Gemmell (Digital Wireless, CEO)	1
154. VoiceXML	Alex Laats (Informio, CEO and Co-Founder)	1
155. Reaching the Epitome of Productivity	Rod Hoo (LGC Wireless, President and CEO)	1
156. Identifying Revenue Opportunities	Scott Bradner (Harvard Univ., Senior Technical Consultant)	1
157. The Wireless Satellite Space	Tom Moore (WildBlue, President and CEO)	1

* **Denotes Best Selling Chapter**

Chapter #/Title	Author	Units
158. *Memory Solutions for Semiconductor Industry	Steven R. Appleton (Micron Technology, Inc., CEO)	1
159. *Programmable Logic: The Digital Revolution	Wim Roelandts (Xilinx, Inc., CEO)	1
160. The Streaming Media Future	Jack Guedj, Ph.D. (Tvia, Inc., President)	1
161. Building a Winning Semiconductor Company	Igor Khandros, Ph.D. (FormFactor, Inc., President and CEO)	1
162. The Next Generation Silicon Lifestyle	Rajeev Madhavan (Magma, Chairman, CEO and President)	1
163. Semiconductors: The Promise of the Future	Steve Hanson (ON Semiconductor, President and CEO)	1
164. Dynamics of the Semiconductor Data Center	Eyal Waldman (Mellanox Technologies, LTD, CEO)	1
165. The Market-Driven Semiconductor Industry	Bob Lynch (Nitronex, President and CEO)	1
166. Semiconductors: Meeting Performance Demand	Satish Gupta (Cradle Technologies, President and CEO)	1
192. Balanced Internet Marketing Programs	Meg Brossy (Chief Marketing Officer, 24/7 Media)	1
193. Internet Ad Campaigns, Not Just Cool Ads	Brooke Correll (Wineshopper.com, VP Marketing)	1
194. Internet Advertising: Moving the Profit Needle	John Herr (Buy.com, Sr. VP Marketing & Advertising)	1
202. Future Internet Opportunities	Joe Krauss (Excite@Home, Founder)	1
203. Internet Future: An International Perspective	Charles Cohen (Beenz.com, CEO)	1
204. Valuing Internet Companies	John Segrich (CIBC, Internet Research Analyst)	1
205. The Potential for Personal Computing	Larry Cotter (Sandbox.com, CEO)	1
206. Using Innovation to Fulfill Customer Needs	Kyle Shannon (AGENCY.COM, Co-Founder)	1
207. Being a Leader in the Internet Economy	Jeff Sheahan (Egghead, CEO)	1
208. *Being a Sustainable Internet Business	Jonathan Nelson (Organic, Inc., CEO and Co-Founder)	1
209. Business-to-Business Effects on the Internet	Chris Vroom (Credit Suisse First Boston, Internet Analyst)	1

* **Denotes Best Selling Chapter**

Chapter #/Title	Author	Units
210. Risk & Uncertainty: Internet Co. Challenges	Joseph Howell (Emusic.com, Chief Financial Officer)	1
211. Focus on Profits in the Internet Economy	Lynn Atchison (Hoovers.com, Chief Financial Officer)	1
212. Cash Flow for Internet Companies	Tim Bixby (LivePerson, Chief Financial Officer)	1
213. Financial Accountability for Internet Companies	Greg Adams (Edgar Online, Chief Financial Officer)	1
214. Establishing Value for Internet Companies	Louis Kanganis (Nerve.com, Chief Financial Officer)	1
215. Managing Rapid Growth	David R. Henkel (Agillion.com, Chief Financial Officer)	1
216. Scalability and Profits for Internet Companies	Alan Breitman (Register.com, Chief Financial Officer)	1
217. *Building Real Value for Internet Companies	Joan Platt (CBS MarketWatch, Chief Financial Officer)	1
218. Financial Forecasting for the Internet Economy	David Gow (Ashford.com, Chief Financial Officer)	1
219. *Organizing the Internet Financial House	Mary Dridi (webMethods, Chief Financial Officer)	1
220. *Internet BizDev: Leveraging Your Value	John Somorjai (Keen.com, VP, Business Development)	1
221. Internet BizDev: Staying Focused	Todd Love (yesmail.com, Senior VP, Business Development)	1
222. Internet BizDev: Focusing on Corporate Goals	Chris Dobbrow (Real Names, SVP, Business Development)	1
223. Finding the Right Partners for an Internet Co.	Scott Wolf (NetCreations, SVP, Business Development)	1
224. Changing Internet Market Conditions	Daniel Conde (Imandi.com, Director, Business Development)	2
225. *Maximizing Time and Efficiencies	Bernie Dietz (WebCT, VP, Business Development)	1
226. Internet BizDev: Pushing the Right Buttons	Mark Bryant (LifeMinders, VP, Business Development)	1
227. BizDev Leadership in the Internet Economy	Robin Phelps (DigitalOwl.com, VP Business Development)	1

FINANCIAL

Chapter #/Title	Author	Units
244. *Merging Information Tech. & Accounting	Paul McDonald (Robert Half Int'l, Executive Director)	1

* Denotes Best Selling Chapter

Chapter #/Title	Author	Units
245. *The Accountant's Perspective	Gerald Burns (Moss Adams, Partner)	2
246. New Areas for Accountants	Dick Eisner (Richard A. Eisner & Co., Managing Partner)	1
247. *Audits & Analyzing Business Processes	Lawrence Rieger (Andersen, Global Managing Partner)	1
248. Accounting & the Entrepreneurial Market	Domenick Esposito (BDO Seidman, Vice Chairman)	1
250. E-Business Transformation	Fred Round (Ernst & Young, Director of eBusiness Tax)	1
251. Accounting: The UK/US Perspective	Colin Cook (KPMG, Head of Transaction Services - London)	1
252. The Changing Role of the Accountant	Jim McKerlie (Ran One, CEO)	1
253. The Future of Accounting	Harry Steinmetz (M.R. Weiser & Company, Partner)	1

INVESTING

Chapter #/Title	Author	Units
197. Who Wants to Become a Millionaire?	Laura Lee Wagner (American Express, Senior Advisor)	1
198. *The Gold is in Your Goals	Harry R. Tyler (Tyler Wealth Counselors, Inc., CEO)	1
199. *Timeless Tips for Building Your Nest Egg	Christopher P. Parr (Financial Advantage, Inc.)	1
200. It's What You Keep, Not Make, That Counts	Jerry Wade (Wade Financial Group, President)	1
201. Accumulating Your Million-Dollar Nest Egg	Marc Singer (Singer Xenos Wealth Management)	1
228. Time-Honored Investment Principles	Marilyn Bergen (CMC Advisors, LLC, Co-President)	1
229. *The Art & Science of Investing	Clark Blackman, II (Post Oak Capital Advisors, Managing Dir.)	1
240. Altering Investment Strategy for Retirement	Gary Mandell (The Mandell Group, President)	1
241. *Fair Value & Unfair Odds in Investing	Scott Opsal (Invista Capital Mngmt, Chief Investment Officer)	1
242. Earnings Count & Risk Hurts	Victoria Collins (Keller Group Investment Mngmnt, Principal)	1

* Denotes Best Selling Chapter

Chapter #/Title	Author	Units
243. *Navigating Turbulent Markets	Howard Weiss (Bank of America, Senior Vice President)	1
249. Building an All-Weather Personalized Portfolio	Sanford Axelroth & Robert Studin (First Financial Group)	1
254. Managing Your Wealth in Any Market	Gilda Borenstein (Merill Lynch, Wealth Mngmt. Advisor)	1
255. Winning Strategies for International Investing	Josephine Jiménez (Montgomery Asset Mngmnt, Principal)	1
256. The Psychology of a Successful Investor	Robert G. Morris (Lord Abbett, Dir. of Equity Investments)	1
257. *Investing for a Sustainable Future	Robert Allan Rikoon (Rikoon-Carret Investments, CEO)	1

OTHER

Chapter #/Title	Author	Units
258. *E-Health: The Adjustment of Internet Tech.	Robert A. Frist, Jr. (HealthStream, CEO and Chairman)	1
259. Health Care: The Paper Trail	Jonathan S. Bush (athenahealth, CEO and Chairman)	1
260. Consumer Backlash in the Health Care Industry	Peter W. Nauert (Ceres Group, CEO and Chairman)	1
261. Forging a Path in the New Health Care Industry	Dr. Norm Payson (Oxford Health, CEO & Chairman)	1
262. The Future of Clinical Trials	Dr. Paul Bleicher (Phase Forward, Chairman)	1
263. Health Care: Linking Everyone Together	John Holton (scheduling.com, CEO)	1
264. The Future of the Health Care Industry	Robert S. Cramer, Jr. (Adam.com, CEO and Chairman)	1
265. Being a Change Agent in Health Care	Kerry Hicks (HealthGrades, CEO & Chairman)	1
266. Personalized Solutions in Health Care	Dr. Mark Leavitt (Medscape, Chairman)	1

* **Denotes Best Selling Chapter**

THE FOCUSBOOK™

ASSEMBLE YOUR OWN BUSINESS BOOK™

Call Us Toll Free at 1-866-Aspatore (277-2867)
Or Tear Out the Next 2 Order Form Pages & Fax or Mail BOTH Pages To:
Aspatore Books, PO Box 883, Bedford, MA 01730
Or Fax To (617) 249-1970 (Preferred)

Name:

Email:

Shipping Address:

City: State: Zip:

Billing Address:

City: State: Zip:

Phone:

Book Content-5 Questions
1. What chapters would you like added? (Please list by number and author last name-i.e. 2-Jones.) (10 Units/Chapters is Standard for 1 Book.):

_____

_____

_____

_____

_____

_____

_____

2. If you are adding content, do you want it put at the beginning or end of the book? _____
3. Would you like the chapters in a particular order? (If this part is not filled out, we shall put them in random order.) If so, please list by author in order from first to last:

_____

_____

_____

4. How would you like your name to read on the cover? (If you would like a company/university/course name added as well, please list it here with your name.): _____
5. What would you like the title of the book to be? (If none is added, we will simply put the information from the previous question.):

_____

To Order, Visit Us At www.Aspatore.com Or
Call Toll Free 1-866-Aspatore (277-2867)

Pricing-3 Steps

1. Quantity:

1 Book – $99   **2 Books** – $198 ($99 Per Book)
5 Books – $445 ($89 Per Book)   **10 Books** – $790 ($79 Per Book)
50 Books – $2,450 ($49 Per Book)   **100 Books** – $3,900 ($39 Per Book)
250 Books – $7,250 ($29 Per Book)   **500 Books** – $10,500 ($21 Per Book)
1000 Books – $15,000 ($15 Per Book) **5000 Books** – $49,750 ($9.95 Per Book)

Number of Books: _____ *Price for Books:* _____

2. Decide the Number of Chapters in Your Book (If you are selecting only 10 units or less, please skip to No. 3-units are based on number of pages-most chapters are 1 unit, however some are more depending on length.)

10 Units (Standard-Approximately 200-250 Pages) – No Extra Charge
15 Units – Please Add $25 Per Book if Ordering Between 1-10 Books, Add $15 Per Book if Ordering 50-250 Books, Add $7.50 Per Book if Ordering 500-5000 Books (So if ordering 50 books, the additional charge would be 50x10=$500)
25 Units – Please Add $75 Per Book if Ordering Between 1-10 Books, Add $25 Per Book if Ordering 50-250 Books, Add $10 Per Book if Ordering 500-5000 Books (So if ordering 50 books, the additional charge would be 50x25=$1,250)

Number of Units: _____ *Price for Additional Chapters:* _____

3. Adding Content (You must order at least 50 books to add content.) (If you are not adding any content, skip this section.)

Adding 1 Page – Please Add $3 Per Book if Ordering 50-250 Books, Please Add $2 Per Book if Ordering 500-5000 Books
Adding 2-9 Pages – Please Add $8 Per Book if Ordering 50-250 Books, Add $4.00 Per Book if Ordering 500-5000 Books
Adding 10-49 Pages – Please Add $18 Per Book if Ordering 50-250 Books, Add $9 Per Book if Ordering 500-5000 Books
Adding 50-99 Pages – Please Add $25 Per Book if Ordering 50-250 Books, Add $13 Per Book if Ordering 500-5000 Books
Adding 100-149 Pages – Please Add $40 Per Book if Ordering 50-250 Books, Add $20 Per Book if Ordering 500-5000 Books

(Please base page count by single spacing, 12 point font, Times New Roman font type on 8.5X11 paper.) (Only charts and graphs that are smaller than 4 inches wide and 7 inches tall can be included.)
(A staff member will email you within 1 week of the order being placed to coordinate receiving the materials electronically.)

Number of Pages Added: _____ *Price for Pages Added:* _____

To Order, Visit Us At www.Aspatore.com Or Call Toll Free 1-866-Aspatore (277-2867)

PLEASE REPRINT THE FOLLOWING INFORMATION FROM THE PREVIOUS PAGE:

Number of Books: _____   *Price for Books:* _____
Number of Units: _____   *Price for Additional Chapters:* _____
Number of Pages Added: _____   *Price for Pages Added:* _____
Total Price From Sections 1-3: _____

(If mailing in a check you can skip this section but please read fine print below and sign below-check must be received before a book is started-please email jennifer@aspatore.com for an alternate address if you are going to send the check via FedEx or UPS as the PO Box will not accept such shipments.)

Credit Card Type (Visa & Mastercard & Amex):

Credit Card Number:

Expiration Date:

Signature (Acceptance of Order and Terms & Conditions): _____

IF ADDING CONTENT, AFTER FAXING/MAILING THIS FORM, PLEASE EMAIL THE CONTENT AS A MICROSOFT WORD ATTACHMENT TO JENNIFER@ASPATORE.COM. THE EMAIL SHOULD INCLUDE YOUR NAME AND FOCUS BOOK NAME. YOU WILL RECEIVE AN EMAIL BACK WITHIN 24 HOURS IF THERE ARE ANY PROBLEMS/QUESTIONS FROM OUR STAFF.

*(Please note the billing address much match the address on file with your credit card company exactly)

For rush orders, guaranteed to ship within 1 week (for orders of 10 books or less) or within 2 weeks (for orders of 50 books or more) please initial here _____. An additional charge of $100 for orders of 10 or less books, $250 for orders of 11-25 books, $500 for orders of 25-100 books will be charged. If additional information is needed on rush orders, please email jennifer@aspatore.com.

If you would like your order sent via FedEx or UPS, for faster delivery, please enter your FedEx or UPS number here: _____ Please Circle One (FedEx/UPS). Delivery Type-Please Circle (Next Day, 2Day/Ground)

FOR QUESTIONS, PLEASE CONTACT ASPATORE BOOKS VIA EMAIL AT STORE@ASPATORE.COM.

Terms & Conditions - Prices include shipping and handling, unless a rush order is placed. All books are sent via media mail. We shall send a confirmation receipt to your email address. If ordering from Massachusetts, please add 5% sales tax on the order. If ordering from outside of the US, an additional $8.95 for shipping and handling costs will be charged for the first book, and $1.95 for each book thereafter. All books are paperback and will be shipped as soon as they become available. Sorry, no returns, refunds or cancellations at any point, even before the order has shipped or any additional content submitted. Aspatore Books is also not liable for any spacing errors in the book-only printing errors as determined by Aspatore Books. Any additions to the book will be formatted in relation to the rest of the text font size and type. Publication dates are subject to delay-please allow 1-4 weeks for delivery.

Please note that the rights to any content added to the Focusbook™ shall be retained by the author, and that Aspatore Books is simply printing the material in the Focusbook™, not publishing it. Aspatore Books shall not print, publish or distribute the content in any other media, or sell or distribute the content. The rights to all other material in the book shall remain the property of Aspatore Books and may not be reproduced or resold under any condition with out the express written consent of Aspatore Books. The author warrants and represents that to the best of his/her knowledge: (a) he/she has the right to print this material; (b) he/she has no contractual commitment of any kind which may prevent him/her from printing the material; (c) the contribution does not contain any unlawful, libelous or defamatory matter and does not infringe upon the rights, including copyright, of any other person or entity. The individual adding content to the Focusbook™ agrees to assume full liability for any content added to their FocusBook™, and agrees to indemnify and hold harmless Aspatore Books, its owners, officers, employees, agents, shareholders, parents, affiliates, subsidiaries, predecessors, agents, legal representatives, successors and assignees from and against any and all suits, claims, damages, liabilities, including attorneys' fees, based on or with respect to the falsity of any representation or warranty made to Aspatore Books, whether actual or claimed, or any infringement or related claims.

To Order, Visit Us At www.Aspatore.com Or Call Toll Free 1-866-Aspatore (277-2867)

Inside the Minds: The Semiconductor Industry-Leading CEOs Share Their Knowledge on the Future of Semiconductors (ISBN: 1587620227)

Inside the Minds: Chief Technology Officers-Developing, Implementing and Capitalizing on the Best Technologies in the World (ISBN: 1587620081)

Bigwig Briefs: Become a CTO-Leading CTOs Reveal How to Get There, Stay There, and Empower Others That Work With You (ISBN: 1587620715)

Bigwig Briefs: Small Business Internet Advisor-Big Business Secrets for Small Business Success on the Internet (ISBN: 1587620189)

Inside the Minds: Internet Marketing-Advertising, Marketing and Building a Successful Brand on the Internet (ISBN: 1587620022)

Inside the Minds: Internet Bigwigs-Leading Internet CEOs and Research Analysts Forecast the Future of the Internet Economy (ISBN: 1587620103)

Inside the Minds: Internet CFOs-Information Every Individual Should Know About the Financial Side of Internet Companies (ISBN: 158762)

Inside the Minds: Internet BizDev-The Golden Rules to Inking Deals in the Internet Industry (ISBN: 1587620057)

Bigwig Briefs: The Golden Rules of the Internet Economy-The Future of the Internet Economy (Even After the Shakedown) (ISBN: 1587620138)

Inside the Minds: Internet Lawyers-Important Answers to Issues For Every Entrepreneur, Lawyer & Anyone With a Web Site (ISBN: 1587620065)

LAW

Inside the Minds: Leading Labor Lawyers-Labor Chairs Reveal the Secrets to the Art & Science of Labor Law (ISBN: 1587621614)

Inside the Minds: Leading Litigators-Litigation Chairs Revel the Secrets to the Art & Science of Litigation (ISBN: 1587621592)

Inside the Minds: Leading IP Lawyers-IP Chairs Reveal the Secrets to the Art & Science of IP Law (ISBN: 1587621606)

Inside the Minds: Leading Deal Makers-Negotiations, Leveraging Your Position and the Art of Deal Making (ISBN: 1587620588)

Inside the Minds: Internet Lawyers-Important Answers to Issues For Every Entrepreneur, Lawyer & Anyone With a Web Site (ISBN: 1587620065)

For More Information, Visit Us At
www.Aspatore.com Or
Call Toll Free 1-866-Aspatore (277-2867)

Bigwig Briefs: The Art of Deal Making-The Secrets to the Deal Making Process (ISBN: 1587621002)

Bigwig Briefs: Career Options for Law School Students-Leading Partners Reveal the Secrets to Choosing the Best Career Path (ISBN: 1587621010)

MARKETING/ADVERTISING/PR

Inside the Minds: Leading Marketers-Leading Chief Marketing Officers Reveal the Secrets to Building a Billion Dollar Brand (ISBN: 1587620537)

Inside the Minds: Leading Advertisers-Advertising CEOs Reveal the Tricks of the Advertising Profession (ISBN: 1587620545)

Inside the Minds: The Art of PR-Leading PR CEOs Reveal the Secrets to the Public Relations Profession (ISBN: 1587620634)

Inside the Minds: PR Visionaries-The Golden Rules of PR and Becoming a Senior Level Advisor With Your Clients (ISBN: 1587621517)

Inside the Minds: Internet Marketing-Advertising, Marketing and Building a Successful Brand on the Internet (ISBN: 1587620022)

Bigwig Briefs: Online Advertising-Successful and Profitable Online Advertising Programs (ISBN: 1587620162)

Bigwig Briefs: Guerrilla Marketing -The Best of Guerrilla Marketing-Big Marketing Ideas For a Small Budget (ISBN: 1587620677)

Bigwig Briefs: Become a VP of Marketing-How to Get There, Stay There, and Empower Others That Work With You (ISBN: 1587620707)

FINANCIAL

Inside the Minds: Leading Accountants-The Golden Rules of Accounting & the Future of the Accounting Industry and Profession (ISBN: 1587620529)

Inside the Minds: Internet CFOs-Information Every Individual Should Know About the Financial Side of Internet Companies (ISBN: 1587620057)

Inside the Minds: The Financial Services Industry-The Future of the Financial Services Industry & Professions (ISBN: 1587620626)

Inside the Minds: Leading Investment Bankers-Leading I-Bankers Reveal the Secrets to the Art & Science of Investment Banking (ISBN: 1587620618)

For More Information, Visit Us At
www.Aspatore.com Or
Call Toll Free 1-866-Aspatore (277-2867)

Bigwig Briefs: Become a CFO-Leading CFOs Reveal How to Get There, Stay There, and Empower Others That Work With You (ISBN: 1587620731)
Bigwig Briefs: Become a VP of Biz Dev-How to Get There, Stay There, and Empower Others That Work With You (ISBN: 1587620723)
Bigwig Briefs: Career Options for MBAs-I-Bankers, Consultants & CEOs Reveal the Secrets to Choosing the Best Career Path (ISBN: 1587621029)

INVESTING

Inside the Minds: Building a $1,000,000 Nest Egg -Simple, Proven Ways for Anyone to Build a $1M Nest Egg On Your Own Terms (ISBN: 1587622157)
Inside the Minds: Leading Wall St. Investors -The Best Investors of Wall Street Reveal the Secrets to Profiting in Any Economy (ISBN: 1587621142)

OTHER

Inside the Minds: The New Health Care Industry-The Future of the Technology Charged Health Care Industry (ISBN: 1587620219)
Inside the Minds: The Real Estate Industry-The Future of Real Estate and Where the Opportunities Will Lie (ISBN: 1587620642)
Inside the Minds: The Telecommunications Industry-Telecommunications Today, Tomorrow and in 2030 (ISBN: 1587620669)
Inside the Minds: The Automotive Industry-Leading CEOs Share Their Knowledge on the Future of the Automotive Industry (ISBN: 1587620650)

For More Information, Visit Us At
www.Aspatore.com Or
Call Toll Free 1-866-Aspatore (277-2867)

ASPATORE

Executive Business Intelligence

BUSINESS BOOKS-ORDER FORM

Call Us Toll Free at 1-866-Aspatore (277-2867)
Or Tear Out This Page and Mail or Fax To:
Aspatore Books, PO Box 883, Bedford, MA 01730
Or Fax To (617) 249-1970 (Preferred)

Name:

E-mail:

Shipping Address:

City: State: Zip:

Billing Address:

City: State: Zip:

Phone:

Please List Titles & Quantity:

_____

_____

_____

_____

_____

_____

Total Number of Books:_____

(If mailing in a check you can skip this section but please read fine print below and sign below)

Credit Card Type (Visa & Mastercard & Amex):

Credit Card Number:

Expiration Date:

Signature:

*(Please note the billing address much match the address on file with your credit card company exactly)

Terms & Conditions-All Inside the Minds titles retail for $27.95, except Leading Labor Lawyers, Leading Litigators, and Leading IP Lawyers, which retail for $37.95. All Bigwig Briefs titles retail for $14.95. All other titles retail for $27.95. A shipping and handling charge of $3.95 per book will be added. If ordering from outside of the US, an additional $8.95 for the first book and $2.95 for each book thereafter will be charged for shipping and handling. Sorry, no returns or refunds or cancellations. Books that are not already published will be shipped upon publication date. Publication dates are subject to delay.

For More Information, Visit Us At
www.Aspatore.com Or
Call Toll Free 1-866-Aspatore (277-2867)

ASPATORE

Executive Business Intelligence